PAUL MENDELSON has written for the theatre and television, has been the bridge columnist for the *Financial Times* for over a quarter of a century, and is the author of fifteen non-fiction titles concerning mind-sports such as bridge and poker, as well as being a crime novelist whose first novel, *The First Rule of Survival*, was short-listed for the CWA Golden Dagger Crime Novel of the Year in 2014. His second novel, *The Serpentine Road*, was long-listed for the same prize in 2015. Both have been translated into several languages and a television adaptation is in preparation. His two subsequent books are *The History of Blood* and *Apostle Lodge*. Paul lives in London and Cape Town with his two- and four-legged family.

Also by Paul Mendelson

The Golden Rules of Bridge
Mendelson's Guide to Duplicate Bridge
Control the Bidding
121 Tips for Better Bridge
Thinking About Bridge
Bridge for Complete Beginners
The Right Way to Play Bridge
Bridge: Winning Ways to Play Your Cards
Texas Hold 'em Poker: Begin and Win
Texas Hold 'em Poker: Win Online
The Mammoth Book of Poker
The Mammoth Book of Casino Games

The First Rule of Survival
The Serpentine Road
The History of Blood
Apostle Lodge

THE JOY OF
BRIDGE

Everything you need to know
to enjoy your game

PAUL MENDLESON

HEAD START

15 Church Road
London SW13 9HE
www.palazzoeditions.com

Paperback ISBN 9781786751379
eBook ISBN 9781786751607

Design and typesetting by Danny Lyle

Printed in the UK

10 9 8 7 6 5 4 3 2 1

Contents

Introduction   **ix**

Declarer Essentials and Techniques   **1**
Make a plan   2
Ruffing losers   4
Suit establishment in suit contracts   13
Loser-on-loser play   23
Two suit combinations: 1 Missing three honours
dilemma; 2 The missing two honours dilemma   27
Planning the play in no-trump contracts   31
Holding up in no-trumps   38
Tempo in no-trumps   45
Entries   51
Finesses: Standard finesses; 2-way
finesses and counting; Discovery play   55
Frozen suits   63
Re-arrangement of finesses   65
One key safety play   66
Avoidance   74
Not drawing trumps   82
Rembering the auction; Counting   88
Train your brain   96
Play out all your trumps   97
Keeping secrets   104
Getting your opponents to help you   108

Defensive Essentials and Techniques   **119**

The three prongs of defence thinking   119

Leading shortages   126

Play the correct card to inform partner   130

What card do you lead in the suit your partner has bid?   131

When <u>not</u> to lead partner's suit   133

Leads against NT contracts   134

Overtaking and jettison   139

Interpret the meaning of your partner's lead   143

Pressure in defence   147

Communicating with partner   152

Showing count   152

Discards   156

The duty of the leader's partner   159

Lead of ace of against NT contracts   161

Covering an honour with an honour – or not   163

Trump promotion   167

Bidding Ideas   **170**

Judging your hand   173

Good bidding is shape-showing   175

Valuing no-trump hands   177

Valuing your hand correctly   181

Which suit to open   183

What should you open with a wildly distributional hand?   187

No-trump bidding with a long minor suit   191

Stopper-showing bids for no-trumps   192

Free bids and forced bids   196

With a weak hand support partner's
major suit with three cards   198
1NT response does not show a balanced hand   200
With a weak hand, support partner's major
suit opposed to re-bidding your minor suit   204
Jump-bidding your opponents' suit; Bidding
your opponents' suit at the 4-level   210
Pudding raises and splinters   217
Roman key-card Blackwood   227
Simple cue-bidding   230
Quantitative raises   235
The reverse   237
Other strong rebids   244
Overcalls and responses   250
Jump overcalls   256
Doubles and responses   260
Responding to a take-out double   262
Unassuming cue-bid in response to a take-out double   264
Doubler's rebid following partner's response   265
Rare use of double to show very strong hands   267
Double of 1NT   268
Bidding gadgets and conventions   272
Stayman   273
Fourth suit forcing   277
What you bid after partner has used 4SF   278
Unusual NT overcall   280

Epilogue   **287**

Introduction

Bridge should be joyous.

It is, quite simply, the most wonderful mind-sport ever invented.

If you are not ecstatically excited each time you sit down to play, you're not doing it right!

You may be an inexperienced player, who is terrified of letting down their partner or even the opponents. Or, you may not like the cut and thrust of competitive bridge… Or, quite possibly, you're hanging out with the wrong crowd – and when it comes to wrong crowds, the bridge world can boast quite the litany of villains, bullies, numbskulls and backbiters.

Bridge is a game. One to be enjoyed for its utter brilliance, and it can be duly enjoyed at any level, whether you and your fellow players have aspirations to compete, or simply enjoy a mind-expanding pastime with your friends and an excuse to eat chocolate.

But, you must be strong. Don't let people bully you, be rude to you, or muck you about. Drop partners and playmates if they aren't supportive (and this includes husbands, wives and parents).

Remove the distractions and revel in this wonderful game.

This book is intended for those who play a little – or a lot – of bridge already. Whether that is kitchen-bridge, after-dinner-sightly-boozy bridge, in-the-garden bridge, gentle duplicate, club duplicate bridge or even high-stake club bridge, this book will hone your skills, improve your thinking and boost your results. How do I know this?

Wherever in the world I am lucky enough to play this wonderful game, I see elements in everyone's game (sadly, including my own) where a little more thought – or, more focused thought – would have made a vital difference. In *The Joy of Bridge*, I want to reflect upon and celebrate everything that is amazing, stimulating and entertaining, but also to help you to develop your own game so that you can derive even more pleasure from it. There is no doubt that, as you get better at bridge, it becomes more and more absorbing, challenging and brilliant.

The simple fact is this: in order both to improve your game and to enjoy it more, you need to stop using your brain to *remember* what to do but, instead, use it to *work out* what to do. That's why there are some very useful principles to understand, even the odd maxim to have in the back of your mind but, really, there needs to be no learning by rote, trying to memorise notes, or follow charts or flippers. So, please read the text carefully, try to focus on the point of the examples and don't stress about remembering any of it – just let it slowly sink in by a process of stress-free osmosis.

Each tip is illustrated with examples, and I have tried to highlight key elements to be thinking about so that, even if you play with lots of partners whose brains don't work as yours will, you will still see the clear improvements in your own game. Some tips may be simple, others more complicated, but there won't be any examples of extreme deals that are unlikely ever to occur in your game, no complex bidding conventions or gadgets, and only basic defensive agreements to try to persuade your partner or regular group of players to play – it will make a huge difference.

If you play bridge with friends who aren't interested in engaging their brains, or who complain if you stop to think, gently explain why it's a good idea to do thinking at the table. If they still object, it's time to meet them in a café for an artisanal, decaffeinated, skinny, goat-milk latte, and keep them away from the green baize.

If you are depressed by the behaviour and attitude of club bridge players, choose a partner or two, promise one another loyalty and support at the table, and ignore everyone else.

Remember that, not only is bridge fascinating and absorbing, it is also good for the brain. Scientific studies are increasingly citing mind-sports as a way to prevent the onset of dementia and brain fuzz.

With the state of the world right now: so much depressing news, along with a miasma of unimaginative, low-quality entertainment on offer, there has never been a better time to play this most thought-provoking, stimulating, sociable and utterly joyous game. I really hope that I can inspire you.

In this book for clarity I've named the four players as: North, East, South and West.

Paul Mendelson
36,000ft over the Atlantic

Declarer Essentials and Techniques

Declarer play is the ultimate *individual* challenge in bridge and is a way that you can improve your knowledge, skills, and results on your own, without having to rely on partner (my partners find that relying on me too often leads to inevitable disappointment).

As you get better, you will be tempted to point out to your partner where he, she, or they, went wrong. Try to resist, at least until after you have finished playing the session. Then, being at your most tactful, wonder aloud at what might have happened on that hand if partner had done, this or that, or the other. It's so much better if you appear to be contemplating the answer yourself, opposed to stating that partner was wrong – and you know better.

In these gender self-identifying times, I have been saved the decision of whether to refer to partner as he or she. In this tome, partners' genders will vary, possibly even changing within the duration of a hand! Sometimes, I might even refer to them as "they" although, tempted as I might be to refer to some of my less-than-favourite partners over the years this way, they will not be described as "it".

Make a plan

When dummy hits the baize, please study it – and the cards in your own hand. Look intelligent. If you play from dummy immediately, everyone will know that you can't be bothered, that you are an unthinking player.

No good bridge player ever plays a card from dummy without some thought.

Let's look at a hand and see what we might be thinking about:

	♠ A43	
	♥ 10932	
	♦ Q4	
	♣ AQ42	
♠ Q85		♠ 106
♥ KQJ75		♥ 86
♦ 972		♦ AJ1065
♣ 108		♣ J973
	♠ KJ972	
	♥ A4	
	♦ K83	
	♣ K65	

N	E	S	W
1NT	NB	3S	NB
4S			

Playing natural systems, South makes a game forcing response of 3S to partner's 1NT opening and is raised to game.

West leads top-of-a-sequence K♥, and down comes the dummy.

What should the declarer be thinking about?

In suit contracts, count your losers in each suit, assuming that suits divide reasonably, but that finesses are losing. Use the hand that is longer in trumps – usually the declarer's hand – as the master hand, and the opposite hand – usually dummy – just for its high cards.

On this deal, the declarer has:

1 loser in spades (the queen); more if they split horribly

1 loser in hearts (the 4)

2 losers in diamonds (you will lose either K♦ or Q♦ to the opponents' A♦, and you will also lose the third diamond in your hand

No losers in clubs.

You have four losers – one more than you can afford. What will you do about it?

There are only two main methods of getting rid of losers:

1. Trump losing cards in the hand with the <u>shorter</u> trumps (usually in dummy).

2. Set up a long suit (usually in dummy), then draw trumps, and discard your losing cards on the winners from your long suit.

Even modest players should recognise that, on this hand, to succeed declarer must push out A♦, and then trump their low diamond loser using one of dummy's low trumps. Only then can declarer afford to draw the trumps.

So, at trick one, South should win with A♥, and not draw the trumps.

Instead, at trick 2, he should lead 3♦ to dummy's Q♦, and East will win with her A♦.

East probably returns a heart which is taken by West's J♥. Perhaps West now leads a low heart, East ruffs with 10♠ and declarer over-ruffs with J♠.

Now, South plays K♦ and 8♦, ruffing the latter in dummy with 3♠. Now – and only now – can declarer afford to draw trumps. He cashes A♠ and plays to K♠ in hand. When Q♠ does not appear, he leaves it out – it will win at any time West wants – and plays off his winners.

He loses only A♦, a heart and Q♠. 4S bid and made.

Very often, when you have to ruff a loser – or losers – in dummy, you must delay drawing any trumps before undertaking the ruffs.

Bear in mind that, if you draw some trumps, "for safety", opponents can gain the lead and play trumps themselves, preventing you from making your ruffs. So, if you need to make ruffs, unless you have lots of trumps in both hands, you probably shouldn't draw any trumps at all before undertaking this task.

Ruffing losers

The example above is a classic example of using dummy's trumps to ruff a loser from hand. However, you need to remain alert to the information you have been given before deciding which loser you might ruff.

Look at this example:

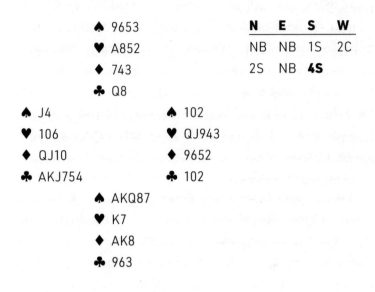

	♠ 9653		**N**	**E**	**S**	**W**
	♥ A852		NB	NB	1S	2C
	♦ 743		2S	NB	**4S**	
	♣ Q8					

West leads A♣ and down comes dummy. You study the table sagely (even if your mind is actually full of thoughts about old love affairs or hot chocolate puddings) and work out that:

You have no losers in spades

You have no losers in hearts

You have one loser in diamonds (the 8♦)

You have three losers in clubs, but it looks as though you can trump the third round in dummy.

The question you must ask yourself is this: Can I safely trump the third round of clubs?

West has overcalled 2C, so he could well hold six of them and, if so, East will play a high club, encouraging West to play K♣ and a third round. It is extremely likely that East will hold either J♠ or 10♠ and overruff dummy's 9♠. If that happens, you will lose the first three tricks and still face a certain diamond loser.

When you play to the first trick, East does play 10♣, and now you know that your predicted scenario will play out. Is there anything you can do about it?

Instead of ruffing the third round of clubs – which we know is dangerous, nay doomed – why not discard 3♦ from the dummy hand? Now, whatever East or West do, nothing can stop you winning the next trick, cashing A♦, K♦ and then playing 8♦ and trumping it in dummy. This is much more likely to be a safe line of play, and neither opponent can ruff in.

By doing this, you make a contract that would otherwise have failed.

This play is called a "Loser Exchange" because you have taken a loser that would have caused you problems (your third club in hand) – because a ruff in dummy would have been overruffed – and exchanged it for a relatively safe loser with which to deal.

8♦ could be overruffed if either opponent had started with a doubleton diamond but, since your opponents held seven diamonds between them, this was relatively unlikely.

Notice that to find this play, you needed to remember the auction (West's 2C overcall), watch the cards the opponents played (East's 10♣ was clearly the higher card from a doubleton), recognise the problem, and then seek a solution.

This is why you need to take your time at trick one and then concentrate as hard as you can for the duration of the deal.

When this deal was first played, declarer went down but, if you make your plan carefully, you should be able to clarify what is actually required, and what is dangerous over-ambition.

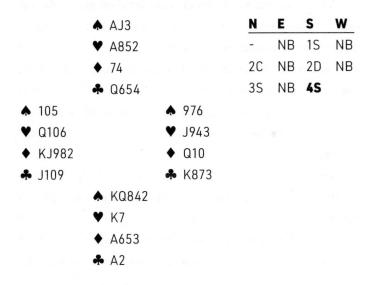

	N	E	S	W
	-	NB	1S	NB
	2C	NB	2D	NB
	3S	NB	**4S**	

♠ AJ3
♥ A852
♦ 74
♣ Q654

♠ 105
♥ Q106
♦ KJ982
♣ J109

♠ 976
♥ J943
♦ Q10
♣ K873

♠ KQ842
♥ K7
♦ A653
♣ A2

3NT would have made but 4S is the more likely spot.
West led J♣. Declarer counted no trump losers, no heart losers, three diamond losers and a club. Correctly, declarer planned to ruff diamond losers with dummy's trumps.

In case West's lead was from something like ♣KJ109, he tried rising with Q♣, but East topped this with K♣, and declarer won with A♣. Knowing that trumps were required for ruffing, trumps were not drawn but, instead, South played A♦ and

3♦, East winning with Q♦. East now switched to 6♠, in an attempt to cut down the number of ruffs South might be able to make.

If the declarer fails to draw trumps straight away,
the defence should definitely consider leading them,
as this is the opposite of declarer's plan.

Declarer won in dummy with J♠, came back to hand with K♥, then led 5♦ and ruffed it with 3♠. East over-ruffed with 9♠ and led his final spade. This removed the last trump from dummy and declarer still has a diamond to lose, meaning that he will lose a club and a total of three diamonds. What was wrong with declarer's plan?

The plan would be fine if South had to ruff two diamonds in dummy; then, ruffing the first loser with a low trump and the second with a high trump makes sense. But, here, only one ruff was required and, to ensure it, declarer should trump with A♠ and then draw trumps. This ensures that the contract is made.

When you require two ruffs, it is usually correct to ruff the first
time with a low trump, the second time with a high trump. But,
when only one ruff is required for success, consider ruffing the
first time with a high trump to ensure there is no over-ruff.

In order to ruff a loser in dummy, you require a shortage to be able to create a void. On this deal, however, declarer had to force her way to make her ruff – and, once again, this relied upon not drawing any trumps herself.

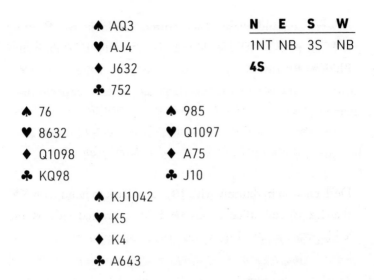

	N	E	S	W
	1NT	NB	3S	NB
	4S			

♠ AQ3
♥ AJ4
♦ J632
♣ 752

♠ 76　　　　　　♠ 985
♥ 8632　　　　　♥ Q1097
♦ Q1098　　　　♦ A75
♣ KQ98　　　　　♣ J10

♠ KJ1042
♥ K5
♦ K4
♣ A643

Playing Natural methods South ended in 4S. West led 10♦. Declarer counted no losers in trumps or hearts, one loser in diamonds (she would score K♦ either at trick 1 or, if East played A♦, later on), and three club losers. With no shortage in dummy, and no promising long suit from which extra tricks might be developed (see Suit Establishment below), it looks as if declarer will have to hope to score J♥, or that the clubs divide 3–3, making her own fourth club into a natural winner. However, this declarer had a more ambitious, but completely logical, method of disposing of one of her club losers.

South played low on West's 10♦, as did East and the trick was won by South's K♦. South now laid down A♣ and followed it with 3♣. East won with J♣ and switched to a trump (there is no hurry to do anything else).

Declarer won this in dummy with Q♠, and led dummy's last club. East didn't trump, but it wouldn't have mattered if East had trumped, since this was a losing trick anyway.

West won and led a second trump. Declarer won this in hand and proudly led her fourth club, ruffing it in dummy with A♠. Finally, she returned to her own hand with K♥ to draw East's last two trumps and, at the end, gave up her diamond loser.

This was the only way to avoid four losers and bring home her game contract.

> *Even without a shortage in dummy, providing that you retain trumps there, you can sometimes force a ruff of a fourth round of the suit by repeatedly playing that long suit until dummy finally runs out.*

One last ruffing example.

Although the dummy usually contains fewer trumps than declarer's hand (or if they both contain the same number, declarer's are usually better quality), sometimes this isn't so.

Playing conventions such as Transfers, or a conventional defence to opponents' 1NT, will often lead you to play in contracts where dummy has more trumps than the declarer's hand. Then you need to remember that, to create extra tricks (or deal with losers) you need to trump in the hand that has the *shorter holding* in trumps.

If you find yourself in this position, it is best to play the deal as what I call an "Upside-down" hand.

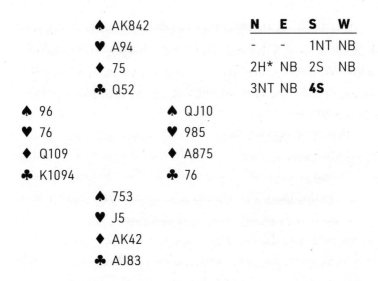

N	E	S	W
-	-	1NT	NB
2H*	NB	2S	NB
3NT	NB	**4S**	

Even if you do not play Transfers yourself, you will find that many people do play them. This example will show you how a declarer thinking clearly will plan the play. From this, you can understand the upside-down thinking and begin to appreciate the best form of defence.

North shows a 5-card spade suit and makes South re-bid 2S. Then, North shows a balanced hand with 13pts or more. Finally South, who is worried about his doubleton heart, converts back to 4S, which is the best game contract.

Because South has revealed a concern about playing in 3NT, West leads a low trump. What should South's plan be?

Rather than just skipping on to the solution, please make your plan now.

When dummy contains more trumps that your (declarer's) hand, you should treat the dummy hand as the master hand and your own hand as, effectively, the dummy. So, calculate your losers in the North hand. In this way, the hand is being played upside-down.

North has one loser in trumps

Two losers in hearts

No losers in diamonds

One loser in clubs (even if the finesse were correct, unless East held precisely ♣Kx, you would still lose the third round).

On this basis, the solution is simple: declarer must trump one heart loser in his own hand (the hand that is shorter in trumps) before drawing all the trumps.

Declarer wins trick 1 in dummy with K♠ and immediately sets about creating a void in his own hand, leading either a low heart first, losing the trick, or cashing A♥ and playing a low heart. Either way, when the opponents win, they should continue leading trumps. Declarer wins in dummy with A♠ and either cashes A♥ – or if this was done already, then leads his third and final low heart from the table and ruffs it with 7♠ in hand. This achieved, declarer will lose K♣ and Q♠ as well as the one heart already lost, and the contract is secured.

We will re-visit this a lot in the section on defence but…

If declarer is trying to create a shortage in the hand with the shorter holding in trumps, planning to make ruffs, the defenders should be leading trumps to try to reduce the declarer's ability to ruff his loser(s).

Suit establishment in suit contracts

The other key method of getting rid of losers is by setting up a long suit in dummy and using the winner(s) established there to discard losers from hand.

I must have played bridge for a good couple of years before anyone explained that this is absolutely the number one declarer technique to try to master.

If the following hands perplex you in any way, please lay out the full deal using playing cards and play through the hand.

Once you master this type of play, your bridge will be transformed.

	N	E	S	W
	–	NB	1H	1S
	2C	NB	2H	NB
	4H			

```
              ♠ J106
              ♥ K52
              ♦ 74
              ♣ AK842
♠ AK954                    ♠ 73
♥ -                        ♥ 10743
♦ KJ1052                   ♦ Q986
♣ 1075                     ♣ QJ6
              ♠ Q82
              ♥ AQJ986
              ♦ A3
              ♣ 93
```

North is pretty frisky raising to 4H but, when West leads A♠ and dummy goes down, declarer must make his plan.

He has three losers in spades because, from his overcall, he knows that West holds at least five of them, so East only holds two at most. Therefore, the defence will begin with A♠, K♠, and a third spade that East will ruff.

There are no losers in hearts

One loser in diamonds

No losers in clubs.

This is one loser too many: what can declarer do to get rid of 3♦ from her hand?

The shortage in dummy is opposite her own shortage, so there is no chance of a ruff. Instead, declarer must try to set up dummy's long suit – clubs – to create a winner on which he can discard 3♦ from his hand.

A♠ is led, followed by K♠ – East signalling her double-ton by playing first 7♠, then 3♠ – and West leads 9♠ which East trumps with 3♥. East then leads 6♦. Declarer must win with A♦.

If he now draws all East's trumps, he will lose a diamond at the end and be defeated.

Instead, he tries to establish the club suit. He plays A♥ and Q♥, carefully preserving K♥ in dummy as an entry for later. Now, he plays a club to dummy's K♣. He cashes A♣ and then plays 2♣. East follows, declarer trumps, and West follows.

If declarer has been counting the club suit, he will know that all the opponents' clubs have now been drawn out – that is what ruffing the third round achieved – and now the two remaining clubs in dummy are both winners. To enjoy them, and to draw East's final trump, declarer plays a low heart to dummy's K♥. Now, he plays 8♣ and discards his losing 3♦ on it. Contract made.

When you try to set up winner in dummy's long suit,
be careful to preserve an entry – or entries – back to
the dummy so that you can enjoy the winner(s).
This may involve delaying drawing all the trumps.

There are hands where you may need more than one entry to establish your long suit.

♠ Q107	
♥ K86	
♦ J4	
♣ AQ543	

N	E	S	W
-	NB	1H	NB
2C	NB	2H	NB
4H			

♠ AK954	♠ 63
♥ 3	♥ 742
♦ 1082	♦ KQ976
♣ 10872	♣ KJ9

♠ J82
♥ AQJ1095
♦ A63
♣ 6

This deal is similar to, but crucially different from, the previous 4H contract.

This time, West has not overcalled 1S and dummy's clubs are not as good.

West leads A♠, K♠ and a third round which East ruffs. East switches to K♦ and, now, declarer faces two diamond losers. He could ruff one in dummy, but that would mean losing another diamond trick to void dummy, and that would give up on making 4H.

Instead, declarer must focus on trying to make three club tricks, so that both diamond losers can be discarded.

Declarer will not be drawing trumps yet, since he is going to need them as entries to dummy.

Having won A♦, declarer plays 6♣ to dummy's A♣, and then 3♣ back, which he ruffs with a high trump in his hand.

Next, he gets back to dummy by playing 5♥ to 8♥, and he plays 4♣, which he also ruffs in his own hand, very pleased that East has produced K♣. This makes his Q♣ a winner and, once that is played, his fifth club in dummy will also be a winner.

Finally, before enjoying his winners, he must draw all the trumps, ending in dummy. He first cashes A♥, and then leads 10♥ to dummy's K♥. All trumps are now drawn, so he plays Q♣, discarding one low diamond from hand, and then 5♣, which is now the last club out, on which he throws his other losing diamond from hand.

If that doesn't seem completely clear to you, please lay out the cards on a table and play it through – suit establishment is crucial to successful bridge and, once you master it, it is not as challenging as it might first appear.

The definition of a long suit is any holding that is longer in one hand than in the other.

You need to remain vigilant for any length disparity that you might be able to exploit for gain…

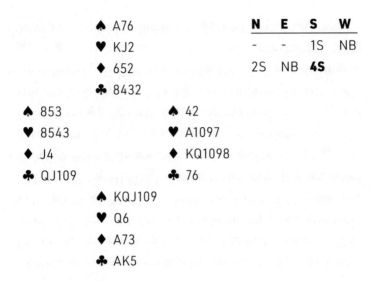

	N	E	S	W
	-	-	1S	NB
	2S	NB	**4S**	

North hand:
- ♠ A76
- ♥ KJ2
- ♦ 652
- ♣ 8432

West hand:
- ♠ 853
- ♥ 8543
- ♦ J4
- ♣ QJ109

East hand:
- ♠ 42
- ♥ A1097
- ♦ KQ1098
- ♣ 76

South hand:
- ♠ KQJ109
- ♥ Q6
- ♦ A73
- ♣ AK5

Holding a weak hand, North correctly raises her partner with 3-card spade support and 4S is reached, instead of the doomed 3NT had North responded 1NT.

West led Q♣ and South made her plan:

She has no loser in spades

One loser in hearts

Two losers in diamonds

And one loser in clubs.

There are no shortages to be utilised in dummy, but is there a long suit?

Yes, the heart suit in dummy is one card longer than in declarer's own hand, and that extra card can be used to discard a loser from hand.

Declarer must not draw any trumps yet, as she will need A♠ as an entry to dummy.

She wins trick 1 with A♣ and immediately plays Q♥ from hand. If East ducks this trick, she continues with 6♥ to J♥ in dummy, and now East must win or declarer has avoided a heart loser. East probably switches to K♦, which South should win. Now, she plays K♠, then Q♠ and finally 9♠ to dummy's A♠. This ensures that all the trumps are drawn before cashing her K♥ winner. She throws either a low club or a low diamond on this, and her loser count is now down to only three. 4S bid and made.

With plenty of trumps in both hands, you can even use a "long" suit in your own hand to discard a low card from dummy, shortening the holding, and allowing a subsequent ruff of a loser in dummy.

	♠ K73	
	♥ A865	
	♦ K2	
	♣ K843	

N	E	S	W
-	NB	1H	NB
3NT*	NB	**4H**	

```
        ♠ K73
        ♥ A865
        ♦ K2
        ♣ K843
♠ QJ104              ♠ 986
♥ 73                 ♥ K2
♦ A1076              ♦ 9854
♣ J92                ♣ A1065
        ♠ A52
        ♥ QJ1094
        ♦ QJ3
        ♣ Q7
```

North's 3NT response to South's 1H opener is a Pudding Raise (see page 217).

South opts to bid the major suit game.

West leads Q♠, and South sees a potential loser in each suit (counting the heart finesse as a loser).

If the trump finesse loses, East would return a spade, exposing the third-round loser and, then, when you pushed out A♣ or A♦, the opponents would cash their spade winner and defeat the contract.

Declarer must set up her spade discard as soon as possible, but there is no long suit in dummy. Instead, South must set up the "long" diamond suit in hand and use that to discard a low spade from dummy. This can then be used to make a spade ruff later on.

Declarer needs to retain an entry into the hand which contains the long suit – her own hand – so she wins trick one with K♠.

She plays ♦K2 and, when West wins, probably on the second round, whether the defender leads a spade or not, declarer can win, get to hand with A♠ and lead a third round of diamonds, throwing away dummy's last spade. Only now can trumps be drawn – losing the finesse – but nothing can prevent declarer from ruffing her last spade in dummy and restricting her losers to just three.

We can conclude from these examples that, when you have too many losers in a suit contract, if you plan either to trump a loser(s) in dummy, or to set up dummy's long suit, you must usually delay drawing your opponents' trumps.

Even though there is a small amount of risk involved in doing this, it must be worth it: you have assessed that, if you do draw the trumps, you have too many losers to succeed, so to take any risk required is, at almost all forms of the game, absolutely correct to give yourself a chance to succeed. Conversely:

> *If, when dummy goes down, you assess that you have few enough losers, that is the time to draw trumps as quickly as possible, so that opponents cannot make adverse ruffs.*

♠ ♥
♦ ♣

I learnt my bridge in the school of very hard (and, for an elderly teenager, very expensive) knocks, at St James's Bridge Club, in London. In the 1960s, 70s and 80s, this was the highest-standard rubber and Chicago bridge club in the UK. Zia Mahmood, Bob Hamman, Robert Sheehan, Claude Rodrigues – these famous internationals would be playing at the next table, for perhaps sixty times the pretty high stakes for which we were playing.

You would enter the club either through the little back entrance in Duke's Street, or via the expansive and grand hallway of the East India Club on St James's Square. It was my dream venue: tables each illuminated by a low-slung, tasselled lampshade, the smell of cigarettes and good cigars, backgammon boards at the ready for some high-stake side action, and always top players to kibbitz. Each session, the club would crack open new decks of cards, and my expectation was at its height.

Over the years, I was given priceless tips, usually in a friendly fashion, by all the players above, plus British internationals Boris Schapiro, Jeremy Flint and Tony Priday. Martin Hoffman and the club's manager, Irving Rose – both geniuses of the game – took me under their wings, just about knocking me into shape. Many a day, I would arrive at the club at 6pm and not leave until 4am the following morning.

I'd like to tell you my story of Mr Ali, an elderly Indian gentleman, with whom I often found myself partnered. I enjoyed playing with Mr Ali, because we both favoured the Weak NT, which wasn't widely played in these circles back in the 1980s. I also liked him as a partner, because he played the hands carefully and thought deeply about the defence. But, the one thing he didn't like was when I stopped to think for a long time about a particular declarer play. Then, he'd shake his head and, in a heavy Indian accent, waving jazz hands, he would cry:

"Oh no, Mr Mendelson. What are you doing? Don't stop to think…" He would say this really quite loudly, so that the whole room could hear. "It's better if you play fast." Then, he'd bow his head, shake it sadly, and bemoan: "It always goes wrong when you *think*…"

I used to enjoy telling that story, even though I didn't really know then – and still don't now – whether he was joking or being completely serious. But, regrettably, my Indian restaurant accent was the problem, so that's another anecdote consigned to the scrapheap.

Recounting this story reminds me of playing with Joe Coral, of the eponymous turf accountancy, who loved his bridge at St James's, and always smoked a huge cigar. He was a slight man with a gammy arm, so I often used to deal for him at his turn. Whenever he picked up poor cards, he would always lean across the table towards his partner, glance at me, and ask:

"Did you see anything?"

The implication being that I'd stacked the deck and diddled him out of a decent hand.

And, then, there was Pat Cotter, former Head of Classics at St Paul's School, who wrote for both the *FT* (*Financial Times*) and *Country Life* magazine for fifty years. His declarer play was excellent, and he was a charming and supportive partner, but he was plagued by average bridge players wanting to feature in one of his columns. If someone was particularly insistent, he would eventually write up the hand, recount the victim's line of play, and then write:

"Now, let's reply the hand together, this time finding a superior line…"

Perhaps the most daunting of all possible partners to draw was the mercurial Rixi Markus, and her jangling charm bracelet which, despite being loaded with gold, platinum and diamonds, to its wearer, wholly failed to impart any charm whatsoever. Make a mistake, and you would be put back on your perch in no uncertain terms.

One evening, she and her partner bid as follows:

1NT – 6NT

The leap to the slam was very much Rixi's style: don't waste time on the bidding, get to the play.

I was on lead and, after some thought, laid down a card. Rixi's partner wrapped up twelve tricks very quickly and I, hoping to benefit from some insight into the expert's mind, asked Mrs Markus if I could have done anything better.

She somehow managed to look down her nose at me despite being two foot shorter than me, and proclaimed in her heavy Eastern European accent:

"You should have listened to the bidding!"

In the context of the deal, it was a meaningless statement, but Rixi had said it, so I nodded appreciatively.

This, after all, was the woman who played with arguably the greatest woman player of all, certainly of her era, Helen Sobel. When asked what it was like to partner the world's best female player, quick as a flash, Rixi pointed across the table, shrugged, and said:"You'd better ask her."

Loser-on-loser play

There are many variations on this standard play – you have already encountered a "Loser Exchange" earlier on – and a loser-on-loser play as an exit manoeuvre in an advanced endplay, but this example illustrates the most common use of this vital play.

As usual at bridge, to find these plays, you need to have immersed yourself in the deal, and remain alert to what your plan is and what your opponents might be scheming. When you are fully focused, you will suddenly discover that you can find these plays and triumph.

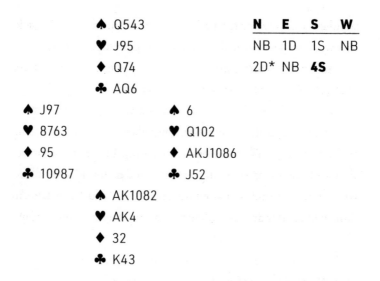

		N	E	S	W
	♠ Q543	NB	1D	1S	NB
	♥ J95	2D*	NB	**4S**	
	♦ Q74				
	♣ AQ6				

♠ J97   ♠ 6
♥ 8763   ♥ Q102
♦ 95   ♦ AKJ1086
♣ 10987   ♣ J52

          ♠ AK1082
          ♥ AK4
          ♦ 32
          ♣ K43

Having passed initially, North's 2D bid is an Unassuming Cue-bid (see page 264), indicating 10pts or more with 3-card support or better for partner's overcalled suit.

Declarer should have only one heart loser and two diamond losers. Her plan is to gain the lead as quickly as possible, and draw out the trumps.

When you hold few enough losers to make your contract,
aim to draw opponents trumps out as quickly as possible

West leads 9♦; dummy plays 4♦, East wins with 10♦ and South plays low. East lays down A♦, to which West follows with 5♦. At trick 3, East leads K♦. What should declarer do?

South should have noted West's lead of 9♦, followed by her play of 5♦, indicating a doubleton. If South trumps in low, West may be able to overtrump with J♠. If South trumps in high, should West have started with three spades headed by the jack, this will promote her jack into a winning trump.

And, there is an additional problem: if she sets up a trick for West, she still has her heart loser to contend with.

You may have found the solution now…

Instead of ruffing, South discards her loser on this losing trick. She drops 4♥. West does not trump but, now, whatever East leads, South can win, draw trumps and claim the rest. If East tries a fourth round of diamonds, because there are now none in dummy also, declarer can safely over-trump anything West plays.

Whenever you feel that you cannot afford to trump high – to prevent an over-ruff – look for a loser in a side-suit you might discard instead.

If we return to the maxim that, if you have few enough losers to make your contract, you should draw trumps as quickly as possible, we should take a quick look at just how quickly one should draw the trumps.

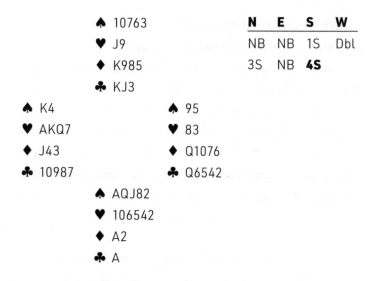

	♠	10763		**N**	**E**	**S**	**W**
	♥	J9		NB	NB	1S	Dbl
	♦	K985		3S	NB	**4S**	
	♣	KJ3					

♠ K4   ♠ 95
♥ AKQ7   ♥ 83
♦ J43   ♦ Q1076
♣ 10987   ♣ Q6542

          ♠ AQJ82
          ♥ 106542
          ♦ A2
          ♣ A

West leads A♥, encouraged by East's 8♥, then K♥ and, at trick 3, 7♥. Declarer ruffs with 10♠ in dummy and this holds the trick. South still has K♠ to lose and a fourth heart, although that can be ruffed quite safely in dummy later.

What should declarer do? If he leads a trump and takes the finesse, this loses to West's K♠, and West leads Q♥. East can over-ruff all the dummy's trumps now, and the contract is defeated.

Declarer should know that West holds K♠, or East would surely have over-ruffed 10♠ in dummy. Now, dummy only holds quite low trumps, that could easily be over-ruffed. So, if declarer remembers the maxim about with few enough losers you draw trumps quickly, he will lead a trump to A♠ in hand and then lead out Q♠. West wins, but now East has no more trumps left and declarer can make his heart ruff in dummy quite safely.

Quickly can therefore really mean quickly, espousing any finesses or other clever stuff, just to ensure your contract.

Two suit combinations
1. Missing three honours dilemma

Here are two examples of playing a suit which seem to defeat the average player but, if mastered, can make a huge difference not only to your results, but also to the way that you think when you look at one suit in isolation.

Imagine that you are faced with trying to make three tricks from this combination of cards:

Q642

W   E

K853

When missing ace, jack, ten – and here, even the nine – you have to aim to make one opponent waste his ace on thin air.

To achieve this, you must guess, or work out, which opponent holds the ace, and then hope that is a doubleton. So, here let's guess that West holds the ace. You would start by leading a low card from your hand – to lead *through* the hand with the key card: if West plays his ace, you play low from dummy, and your king and queen draw the remaining cards – and you score the fourth round too.

If the suit splits 4–1, you were doomed from the start.

If, at trick 1, West correctly plays low, you win with the queen and now you lead a low card from dummy and whatever card East plays, you also play low from your hand. If West did start with a doubleton, his ace is now a singleton and he will have to win with it. This leaves your own king to draw out the last card from East's hand.

If the ace if not a doubleton, you cannot make three tricks.

Let's see this technique in action:

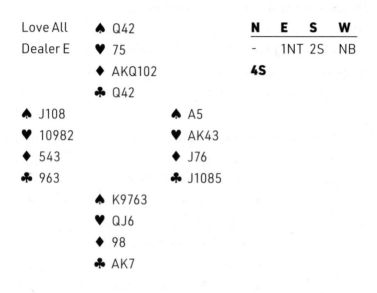

Love All   ♠ Q42 | **N** | **E** | **S** | **W** |
Dealer E   ♥ 75 | - | 1NT | 2S | NB |
                ♦ AKQ102 | **4S** | | | |
                ♣ Q42

♠ J108   ♠ A5
♥ 10982   ♥ AK43
♦ 543   ♦ J76
♣ 963   ♣ J1085

                ♠ K9763
                ♥ QJ6
                ♦ 98
                ♣ AK7

South overcalls with a slightly dodgy suit, but is raised to game rapidly by North. West leads 10♥ and East takes K♥ and A♥, before switching to J♣.

Declarer must only lose one trump trick or will go down. Here, declarer has counted that she and her partner hold 26pts between them, so East must hold 12–14 of the remaining 14pts to justify his 1NT opening. Therefore, East definitely holds A♠. Hoping that it is a doubleton, declarer puts her mind to the correct way to play the trump suit.

She wins the club switch with Q♣ in dummy and leads 2♠. This ensures that she is playing *through* the hand with A♠. East plays low and South wins with her K♠. Now, she leads 3♠ from hand and, even when West plays J♠, she ducks in dummy. East's A♠ takes thin air.

Whatever East leads now, declarer wins, cashes dummy's Q♠, and the rest are hers. Contract made.

2. The missing two honours dilemma

This problem occurs frequently and is considered pretty much trivial by experts, but usually foxes ordinary bridge players.

Let's look at the suit in question:

10984

W   E

AK632

You lay down the ace and West produces the queen, and East the 5. What do you do now?

Do you play the king and hope that the jack falls?

Or do you go over to dummy, lead the ten and, if East plays low, you play low too, finessing East for the jack?

The odds clearly favour the latter option.

At the start of the hand, there is a 25% chance that East holds both queen and jack; there is a 25% chance that West holds both queen and jack; and there is a 50% chance that the honours are split between the two opponents.

Now, once West shows up with the queen, the odds change.

East can no longer hold both queen and jack, so you are left with:

A 25% chance that West holds both queen and jack, and

A 50% chance that the honours were split between the opponents.

Therefore, it is 2 to 1 that East holds the other honour.

As a very general guide, assume that with two honours missing, they are split between the opponents' hands.

Let's see an example from real life that cropped up online just yesterday!

West led 10♠; declarer assessed more than three potential losers.

Game All	♠ KQ64			**N**	**E**	**S**	**W**
Dealer S	♥ 109753			-	-	1H	NB
	♦ Q103			**4H**			
	♣ 7						

♠ 109832		♠ A7
♥ J		♥ Q64
♦ KJ94		♦ 85
♣ J63		♣ AQ9542

♠ J5
♥ AK82
♦ A762
♣ K108

Some of the unknowns were revealed when, having played K♠ and lost to A♠, East switched to 8♦, which declarer ran to West's K♦. Now, there is just A♣ to lose and trumps to sort out.

Winning 9♠ continuation in hand with J♠, declarer laid down A♥, and West dropped J♥.

As we have seen, it might be that West holds ♥QJ doubleton, but it is twice as likely that East holds Q♥.

Unless the bidding has revealed West to hold a balanced hand, or promised a high point-count, declarer should cross to dummy's Q♦ and lead 10♥: when East plays low, South should finesse. This will work at least two thirds of the time.

It is amazing that, of the 23 pairs who had played this hand previously, only five had made it. All of those played the heart suit correctly.

If West had opened 1NT, you would play for her to have ♥QJ doubleton, since she would not (one hopes) have opened 1NT with a singleton jack but, other than this situation, you should finesse for the missing honour if you can.

Planning the play in no-trump contracts

The preparation before you touch dummy is vital in any contract but, perhaps, especially in no-trumps. There is usually one successful line of play and, if you miss it, you'll be doomed.

Let's see what you think here:

	♠ QJ3
	♥ 65
	♦ KQJ102
	♣ 642

N	E	S	W
NB	NB	1H	NB
2D	NB	**3NT**	

6♠ led

♠ A82
♥ AJ84
♦ 83
♣ AKQ7

South could have opened 1C; I prefer 1H on these hands. North is just strong enough to respond at the 2-level and South, with 18pts happily rebids 3NT.

In no-trumps, you count your top tricks and then decide from which suit(s) you will hunt for the extra ones required.

So, here we go:

One top trick in spades

One in hearts

None in diamonds

Three in clubs.

That is five tricks and, once A♦ has been dislodged, you should make four extra tricks there. You also have a second spade trick that will likely be yours too.

Next, take time to analyse the lead. West's 6♠ looks like a fourth highest lead, so he has a top honour at the head of his suit.

Unless there is evidence to the contrary, always assume that the leader against a NT contract has led from a 5-card suit.

Then, count out the suit around the table:

West has five; dummy holds three, declarer holds three, so East holds only two.

Even if West holds six spades, or only four, this calculation will stand you in good stead.

Lastly, you need to consider entries into the hand that contains the long suit, and remember the mantra:

*Always preserve entries into the hand that contains
the long suit which you plan to utilise*

So, what do you do at trick 1?

If you decided to rise with Q♠ or J♠, you will now go down in your game contract!

Yes, you'll make a quick extra spade trick, but when you play on diamonds, East will win his A♦ on the second round, leaving you with none in hand, and when a spade is returned, either you will rise with your A♠, setting up all the rest of West's spades, or if you play low, West will win and play another spade, and you will never reach dummy again.

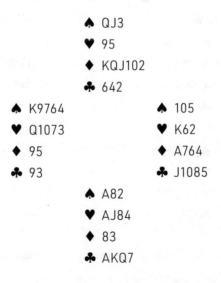

```
                    ♠ QJ3
                    ♥ 95
                    ♦ KQJ102
                    ♣ 642
        ♠ K9764                 ♠ 105
        ♥ Q1073                 ♥ K62
        ♦ 95                    ♦ A764
        ♣ 93                    ♣ J1085
                    ♠ A82
                    ♥ AJ84
                    ♦ 83
                    ♣ AKQ7
```

What went wrong?

Simply, you didn't preserve your entries into the hand that contains the long suit you wished to utilise. Let's re-play the hand remembering that.

At trick 1, play low from dummy and win A♠. This preserves both Q♠ and J♠ on the table, one of which must be an entry. Now, play on diamonds; East will probably still win on the second round. Whether East returns a spade, or switches to a club or a heart, you have time to lead spades twice and, eventually, reach dummy to cash your three diamond winners. Nine or ten tricks will result.

Now, try this one:

	♠ K10943	**N**	**E**	**S**	**W**
	♥ 953	–	NB	1D	NB
	♦ 87	1S	NB	**3NT**	
	♣ A4				

6♥ led

♠ AQ
♥ AQ4
♦ A9652
♣ K97

You have three top spade tricks. On this lead, two heart tricks, one diamond trick and two club tricks – that is eight tricks. Assuming that West's lead is from a 5-card suit, East is marked with two hearts in hand.

The best hope of securing your ninth trick is surely making an extra trick from spades.

What will be your plan?

When I set this hand in class, most students win trick 1 with Q♥ then lead A♠ and Q♠, playing low from dummy each time. They cross to dummy's A♣ and cash K♠. However, since East still holds J♠, that is the end of the suit, and the contract fails.

You only need one extra trick and the best way to aim for that is to play the spades differently.

Win Q♥, cash A♠, and lead Q♠, overtaking it in dummy with K♠. Next, play 10♠ and continue playing them until East wins his J♠. Whatever East returns – probably a heart – you can still reach dummy with A♣ to enjoy the remaining spade winner(s).

Nine tricks safely made.

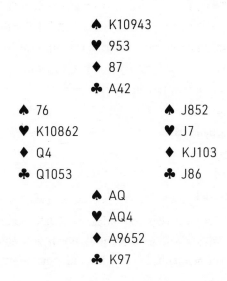

```
                    ♠ K10943
                    ♥ 953
                    ♦ 87
                    ♣ A42
    ♠ 76                        ♠ J852
    ♥ K10862                    ♥ J7
    ♦ Q4                        ♦ KJ103
    ♣ Q1053                     ♣ J86
                    ♠ AQ
                    ♥ AQ4
                    ♦ A9652
                    ♣ K97
```

If you had needed to score all five spade tricks, to play ♠AQ and then cross to A♣ and lay down K♠ is the best line but, here, you only require four spade tricks. By playing this way, you almost guarantee success.

One last little tester for you:

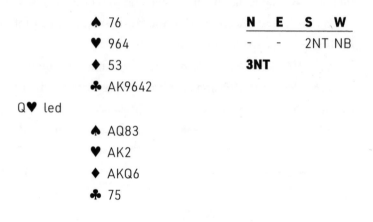

	♠	76		**N**	**E**	**S**	**W**
	♥	964		-	-		2NT NB
	♦	53		**3NT**			
	♣	AK9642					

Q♥ led

♠ AQ83
♥ AK2
♦ AKQ6
♣ 75

If you know this trick – and I imagine that most of you will – it is such an easy problem but, if you don't know it, you need to. So here it is: Duck to retain entry.

You have one spade trick
Two heart tricks
Three diamonds
And two club tricks.

That is eight top tricks. You need only one more. The place to get it is from the club suit, but you have no outside entry. What will you do?

Win trick 1 with K♥ and lead 5♣. West plays J♣. Duck in dummy. Leave West winning the trick. With five clubs out against you, one opponent must hold at least three clubs, so let them win the trick now while you still have a club in your hand to return to dummy.

West probably continues with J♥. You win, and lead a second club to dummy's K♣. When both opponents follow, you lay down A♣ and claim all the club tricks.

	♠ 76		N	E	S	W
	♥ 964		-	-	2NT	NB
	♦ 53		**3NT**			
	♣ AK9642					

♠ K94		♠ J1052
♥ QJ1083		♥ 75
♦ 872		♦ J1094
♣ QJ		♣ 1083

	♠ AQ83
	♥ AK2
	♦ AKQ6
	♣ 75

Should the club suit divide 4–1 or 5–0, you will discover this on the second or first round respectively, and then you can use your second club from hand to reach dummy, cash ♣AK and then try the spade finesse for your ninth trick.

Holding up in no-trumps

Almost everyone knows about holding up in no-trumps. In this short section, we see why, and look at a few exceptions.

♠ AJ3		**N**	**E**	**S**	**W**
♥ 853		-	-	1NT	NB
♦ A9		**3NT**			
♣ KJ642					

6♥ led

♠ 72
♥ A102
♦ KQJ
♣ Q1083

Once you have dislodged A♣, you have nine tricks.

You assume that West has led from a 5-card heart suit, and count out the suit. This leaves East with two hearts.

Assuming that the led suit is splitting poorly, the purpose of the hold-up is to exhaust one opponent of their supply of the led suit, cutting communications between partners.

Here, therefore, declarer ducks the first round of hearts, but wins the second round.

There is nothing to be gained by ducking the second round of hearts since, if hearts are dividing 5–2, to win on the second round has exhausted East of her hearts, and if hearts are dividing 4–3, there are no problems: you cannot lose more than three hearts and A♣.

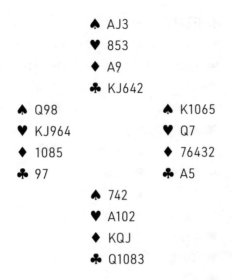

♠ AJ3
♥ 853
♦ A9
♣ KJ642

♠ Q98
♥ KJ964
♦ 1085
♣ 97

♠ K1065
♥ Q7
♦ 76432
♣ A5

♠ 742
♥ A102
♦ KQJ
♣ Q1083

There is an added risk in not winning on the second round, and that is a possible switch by West. Imagine that West at trick 3, feeling that she will not regain the lead, decides to try leading a spade. What do you do now? You have already lost two tricks and you could easily lose three in spades when you dislodge A♣. An easy hand has just turned into a nightmare.

What about this hand?

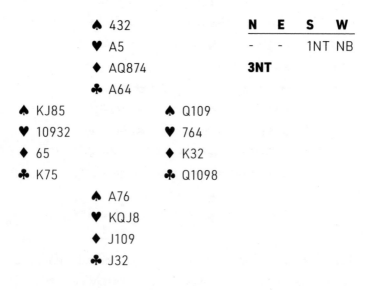

♠ 432
♥ A5
♦ AQ874
♣ A64

N	E	S	W
-	-	1NT	NB
3NT			

♠ KJ85
♥ 10932
♦ 65
♣ K75

♠ Q109
♥ 764
♦ K32
♣ Q1098

♠ A76
♥ KQJ8
♦ J109
♣ J32

West leads 5♠ and declarer counts six tricks outside diamonds so, whether or not the finesse works, there will be at least four more on their way.

What to do about the lead? Normally, reckoning on West holding five spades and East therefore only two, you would duck the first spade trick and win the second. But, here, if your opponents are using standard fourth highest leads, West's 5♠ is the lowest he can hold (everyone can see the ♠432 in dummy), marking him with exactly a 4-card spade suit.

If you duck the first spade, East might switch to a club, and then you would face a whole new set of problems.

East might find this defence: she knows that her partner only holds four spades and, if she counts her tricks in defence, will work out that scoring two or three spade tricks plus K♦, will not defeat the contract. Since she is certain to gain the lead with K♦, she tries to set up her own long suit – clubs. If she correctly switches to 10♣, whatever South does will not prevent East-West from scoring three club tricks, K♦ and the spade trick which was incorrectly ducked at trick 1.

> *Before making a standard hold-up play, check the lead and analyse whether if you duck, is there a suit equally, or even more, dangerous to which your opponents might switch. If so, consider winning immediately.*

In this example, you need to think about the lead very carefully.

♠ A5	**N**	**E**	**S**	**W**

♠ A5
♥ KJ5
♦ 9863
♣ KQ74

N	**E**	**S**	**W**
	-	1NT	NB
3NT			

7♠ led

♠ 9432
♥ AQ7
♦ AK
♣ J1032

Once declarer has pushed out A♣, she will have nine winners, but can she survive the attack in spades?

Assume that West holds five spades, you hold four, dummy two, and so East holds only two also. Normally, then, you would duck the first spade and win the continuation. There are no other suits which you fear the opponents attacking.

However, there is one last factor to consider: where are all the spade honours?

East-West hold K♠, Q♠, J♠ and 10♠ between them and, as West has not led one, he cannot hold more than two of the honours (see page 134).

Therefore, East holds two honours – a doubleton honour – and this gives you a chance to block the spade suit for your opponents completely. Rise with A♠ at trick 1, sit back and watch East-West squirm...

	♠ A5	
	♥ KJ5	
	♦ 9863	
	♣ KQ74	

N	E	S	W
-	-	1NT	NB
3NT			

♠ Q10876		♠ KJ
♥ 1086		♥ 9432
♦ 542		♦ QJ107
♣ A5		♣ 986

	♠ 9432	
	♥ AQ7	
	♦ AK	
	♣ J1032	

If East plays J♠ at trick 1, the next time the opponents lead spades, East will win perforce with K♠ and not be able to play back another. If East drops K♠ under dummy's A♠ (as she probably should) when West leads another spade, either East wins with J♠ and can't lead any more, or West leads Q♠, crashing East's J♠ and setting up your 9♠ in hand as a winner on the fourth round.

You can place any two spade honours in either hand and this will be true.

Notice also that, if you duck trick 1, East wins with K♠ and returns J♠, which you have to win and, now, when West takes A♣, she will have three more spade tricks to take.

If you are missing four or five honour cards in a suit and your opponent leads a low card in that suit, you can assume that he does not hold a sequence or broken sequence of honours, and the honour cards are divided between your opponents' hands.

Finally, let's see a hold-up in action which you might not think is required:

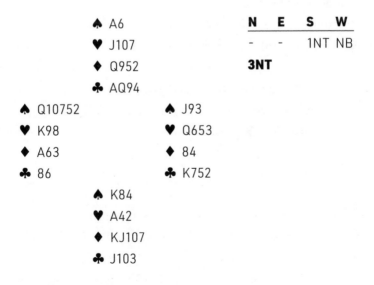

	♠ A6		**N**	**E**	**S**	**W**
	♥ J107		-	-	1NT	NB
	♦ Q952		**3NT**			
	♣ AQ94					

♠ Q10752		♠ J93
♥ K98		♥ Q653
♦ A63		♦ 84
♣ 86		♣ K752

	♠ K84
	♥ A42
	♦ KJ107
	♣ J103

West leads 5♠. Declarer counts only 4 top tricks. He will need extra tricks from both the diamond suit and the club suit. He has two stoppers in the led suit: does he win or duck the first round of spades?

Assuming that West has led from a 5-card suit, East is marked with three spades.

Ideally, when declarer takes the club finesse, he wants East to have run out of spades.

At trick 1, therefore, declarer plays a low spade from both the dummy and his own hand, allowing East's J♠ to win. When East returns 9♠, A♠ wins in dummy, and declarer now plays on diamonds to push out the ace. West wins reluctantly and leads a third spade. Declarer discards a heart from dummy and wins this in hand. Now, he takes the club finesse. East wins but, exactly as planned, East has no spades left to lead and the contract is secured.

Notice that the club finesse was wrong and the spades split badly, yet you still made your contract safely.

When, potentially, you will have to lose the lead twice to make your contract, even with two stoppers in the led suit, consider ducking the first round.

Tempo in no-trumps

Many no-trump contracts are a simple battle between declarer and defence to see which side can establish their suit first. This means that, on many hands, the *tempo* (timing) is vital:

	♠ AJ2	**N**	**E**	**S**	**W**
	♥ 765	-	-	1NT	NB
	♦ AQ982	**3NT**			
	♣ Q4				

5♠ led

♠ Q64
♥ A42
♦ J107
♣ AK73

This 3NT contract requires nothing more than clear thinking to ensure success. West leads 5♠.

Declarer has one spade trick, one heart, one diamond and three clubs: six tricks. Whether or not the finesse works, the diamond suit must produce at least three extra tricks. So, what do you do?

5♠ is clearly a fourth-highest lead so, assume that West holds five spades and East two. To make three spade tricks, you just have to play low from dummy and win trick 1 with Q♠, later finessing West for K♠ with which he's marked.

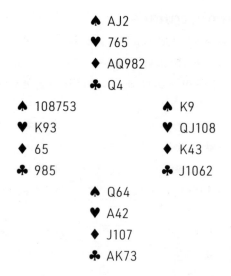

♠ AJ2
♥ 765
♦ AQ982
♣ Q4

♠ 108753   ♠ K9
♥ K93   ♥ QJ108
♦ 65   ♦ K43
♣ 985   ♣ J1062

♠ Q64
♥ A42
♦ J107
♣ AK73

That plan goes horribly wrong when East unexpectedly turns up with K♠. He wins the first trick and switches to Q♥. Whether or not declarer hops up with A♥, West unblocks K♥ at his first opportunity and returns 9♥. When declarer later takes the diamond finesse, East wins K♦ and cashes his heart winner(s). One down.

Did you notice what happened? We made our plan, but then diverted from the path of the righteous, and wondered down the dark alley of making-three-spade-tricks. *That wasn't part of the plan.*

You have two stoppers in spades whoever holds K♠ but, to secure nine tricks, you just have to ensure that you still have A♥ in hand when you take the diamond finesse. To play this way, at trick 1, rise with A♠ in dummy. Cash Q♣, and come to hand with K♣. Now, lead J♦ and, when West follows low, play low from dummy. East may play hard-to-get and duck the first finesse, but simply persevere. When East does win with K♦, he can switch to a heart or return a spade, but you are in control of every suit.

Wait a minute! I hear some of you say: West's lead was wrong. He didn't have a top honour: he should have led 8♠. And, you're right, but welcome to the real world where people play differently to you, don't know the correct lead, or have just pulled out the wrong card because they have plum jam on their middle finger (that's an excuse genuinely used against me)!

Your job is to cut through all the excuses, ignorance and carelessness and find the best way to establish your long suit in no-trumps.

			N	E	S	W
♠	K4		NB	NB	1C	1S
♥	J9752		2H	NB	**3NT**	
♦	K1093					
♣	Q10					

J♠ led

♠ AQ
♥ Q103
♦ J64
♣ AKJ65

Since North's 2H response promises five hearts, South might have rebid 4H, but he felt that his ♠AQ would be more useful in no-trumps, with the lead emanating initially from West. West leads J♠. Put yourself in the declarer's shoes: how should South play the hand?

Declarer has two spade tricks, no hearts, no diamonds and five clubs. You require two extra tricks. From where will they be found?

Initially, your eye will be drawn to the heart suit. Generally, you attack your longest suit. But, here again, there is a timing issue. When you win trick 1, you have only one spade stopper remaining and, in hearts, you will have to dislodge both the ace and king. When you lose the first, spades will be continued, knocking out your last stopper. When you lose a second top heart, your opponents will cash all their spade winners. You will lose two hearts, four spades and A♦ – that'll be three down!

Now, seek a plan that is not doomed to failure…

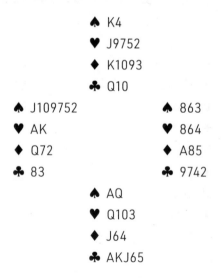

Since you require only two extra tricks, the diamond suit might be able to provide for you. Obviously, you have to lose A♦ but, if West holds Q♦, you will definitely score two extra tricks, providing you lead through West repeatedly.

Win trick 1 with Q♠ in hand and immediately advance J♦. West probably shouldn't cover, so you play low from dummy. East probably pounces with his A♦ and returns 8♠. Unless East has done something very strange, this marks West with Q♦. You win A♠ and lead 4♦. When West plays low again, you finesse with 9♦. This holds so, now, cash Q♣, return to hand and enjoy all the clubs, before leading 6♦. West's Q♦ appears, so you can win in dummy and enjoy 10♦ also.

3NT made with an overtrick, opposed to failing by three tricks – quite a difference, achieved with only a little extra thought.

I include this next hand, because whenever I set it, students fail the test. See how you would do.

♠ 753			
♥ K64			
♦ 9543			
♣ 742			

N	E	S	W
-	-	2C	NB
2D	NB	2NT	NB
3NT			

3♥ led

♠ AK2
♥ A85
♦ AKQJ
♣ K65

You have eight top tricks. From where will the ninth come?

I have watched so many times as declarers win on the first or second round of hearts (second is probably best) and then cash four rounds of diamonds – which could, possibly help – and then hope that the opponents mis-defend. Sometimes, they do. More often, however, West discards J♣ at his first turn: a high card suggesting that he wants a spade led next. East hangs onto spades and throws a club. That has only allowed East-West to communicate via signals, making a defensive mistake less likely.

The only thing that matters here is to realise that K♣ is declarer's only hope of a ninth trick and, to that end, when you win with K♥, you must lead a low club from dummy towards your king, hoping that East holds A♣. If West holds it, you will go down – but West should never be leading away from an ace around into a very strong hand anyway so, if you don't play clubs, West never should. If East holds A♣, he should never lead it, or away from it, and eventually, you'll have to play clubs from your own hand.

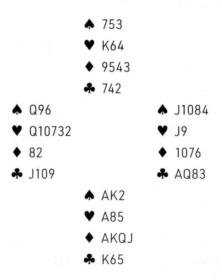

	♠ 753	
	♥ K64	
	♦ 9543	
	♣ 742	
♠ Q96		♠ J1084
♥ Q10732		♥ J9
♦ 82		♦ 1076
♣ J109		♣ AQ83
	♠ AK2	
	♥ A85	
	♦ AKQJ	
	♣ K65	

In my view, the best line of play is to duck the lead and win the continuation with K♥ in dummy. Lead 2♣ now and, if East plays low, place K♣ firmly on the table. When this holds the trick, you have your contract.

If you have only one hope of making an extra trick, take it, even if you might fail by more tricks if it doesn't work.

Entries

As I hope you have observed in many of the preceding examples, entries (sometimes referred to as "means of access", or "transportation") are crucial if you are going to be successful in setting up a long suit, and even sometimes when ruffing losers in the hand that is shorter in trumps.

In the next example, there is only one realistic hope of making the contract, but such a plan relies on carefully creating an extra entry to the dummy hand.

	♠ A643	
	♥ 1032	
	♦ 652	
	♣ 1043	

♠ J72		♠ 98
♥ 84		♥ K9765
♦ KQ109		♦ A83
♣ QJ92		♣ 765

	♠ KQ105	
	♥ AQJ	
	♦ J74	
	♣ AK8	

N	E	S	W
-	NB	2NT	NB
3NT			

North raises South's 20–22pt 2NT opener to 3NT because he holds 4pts for his A♠, and two half points for his 10♥ and 10♦ (although, in this case, neither prove useful). In NT contracts tens, and even nines, can make a huge difference to your chances.

When West leads K♦, declarer realises that he may lose five diamond tricks straight away but, in case the opponents can only take four tricks (as they do here) he makes his plan to make the remaining nine tricks.

He has four spade tricks;

One heart trick

No diamonds

And two club tricks.

If the heart finesse is correct, he can add two more heart tricks to these totals.

However, there is a problem: how do you reach dummy twice to take the heart finesse twice? The A♠ is one obvious entry, but the other one is hidden.

Let's play the hand together:

West leads K♦, and East correctly overtakes with A♦ and returns 8♦ (for more information on why this is the correct play, see "Overtaking and jettison" on page 139).

West wins this second trick and then cashes his two further diamond winners, before getting off lead safely by leading Q♣.

Now, you should play K♠ and Q♠. When both opponents follow, you know that the suit is dividing 3–2. For the third round of spades, lead 10♠ from hand, and overtake this with A♠ in dummy. Now, lead a low heart and, when East follows low, finesse with J♥. It holds. Finally, you can cross over to dummy using your carefully preserved 5♠ to dummy's 6♠! This gets you on the table and able to lead a second low heart. When East pays low again, you play Q♥ and, again, it wins. Together with ♣AK and A♥ you now have nine tricks.

	♠ 432			N	E	S	W
	♥ 8763			NB	NB	1H	NB
	♦ AJ			2H	NB	**4H**	
	♣ 10543						

	♠ QJ9		♠ K1076
	♥ 54		♥ A2
	♦ Q9653		♦ 10874
	♣ 762		♣ K98

	♠ A85
	♥ KQJ109
	♦ K2
	♣ AQJ

South might well have opened 2NT and North would probably have raised to 3NT. On the lead of 5♦, declarer would have had time to do what was necessary to make ten tricks.

Against 4H, West decided to lead Q♠.

What is your plan to score ten tricks now?

You have two losers in spades, a loser in hearts and a club loser (you always count finesse as losers).

You have only one realistic plan and that is to take the club finesse twice. How can you reach the table twice to make that play?

You probably win trick 1 with A♠ and lead a trump. East will win and return 7♠ to West's 9♠. West cashes J♠ and, then, with no long suit in dummy and realising that there is therefore no hurry to take tricks, gets off lead with his other trump.

Declarer wins this in hand and now goes for broke to make his contract.

He leads 2♦ and, when West follows low, he finesses with J♦!

When this holds the trick, he leads a low club from dummy and, when East plays low, he puts in Q♣ – and that holds the trick. He can now return to dummy for the second time by playing K♦ to A♦ and lead a second club, inserting J♣ after East plays low. When this also wins, declarer loses no more tricks and make his contract.

There is an expert observation about the defence this deal: West can thwart declarer's plan by rising with Q♦ on the first round of diamonds, but you'd have to be a very good player to spot that one.

♠ ♥
♦ ♣

Albert Benjamin, the charismatic and brilliant Scottish International player, who invented Benjaminised Acol, was a very witty man. I remember him explaining why he'd given up directing big duplicate competitions. He said that most people never listened to a word he said, complained about his rulings and were, generally, jolly rude.

In these big bridge events, there might 200 tables of players, all moving from one table to another every half hour or so.

Inevitably, some people couldn't find the table for which they were destined.

On this occasion, two ladies, both out of breath and red in the face, called him to the edge of the playing area.

"We're lost," they panted. "Where do we go?"

Albert knew that the solution would be easy. He just had to ascertain at which table they had just played.

"Where have you come from?" he asked.

"The toilets."

Without missing a beat. "And before that?"

The ladies looked at one another, vaguely perplexed.

"Solihull."

Finesses

If you cannot establish a long suit or ruff losers in the hand that is shorter in trumps, you will have to rely on a combination of luck and skill when you play your suits. Knowing some of the key techniques will really help you here.

You must be clear what your ambition is for each situation and then plan a way to give yourself the best chance of achieving it.

Standard finesses

a)	AQ64		b)	AQ83	
K95		J107	K764		92
	832			J105	

c)	AJ84		d)	Q764	
K9		1076	K7		J109
	Q532			A832	

e)	AJ63		f)	AJ65	
Q94		10	1083		Q9
	K8752			K742	

In each example, you are the declarer, sitting South: dummy is North.

a) You would like to make two tricks. The ace is one trick and your only hope of a second is to make the queen. You must lead towards the card you are hoping score.

Lead a low card from hand and, when West follows low, put in the queen. It holds.

If East has the king, you will lose, but this is your best chance.

b) This is the same as above but, because you also hold the jack and ten, you are aiming to make at least three tricks, maybe all four. To retain the lead in your hand, lead the jack first and, if West plays low, play low from dummy also, and continue with the ten.

If West covers the jack with the king, win with dummy's ace and then play low to the ten in your hand. With East holding the doubleton nine, you will make all four tricks.

You can, however, only lead an honour card for a finesse if you also hold at least one touching card. If not, lead a low card.

c) You are trying to capture West's king (if he holds it) and make all four tricks but, as you do not hold the king, ten or nine, your only hope of doing so is to play that, not only does West hold the king, but it is a doubleton. Therefore, lead a low card from hand and finesse with the jack in dummy, then cash the ace. Here, the king falls and you lose no tricks.

If you lead the queen from hand, West will cover with the king and East will score his ten on the third round.

d) Despite missing king, jack, ten and nine, you are aiming to make three out of the four tricks here. To succeed, you must score a trick with the queen. You can cash the ace first if you wish but, ultimately, the key play is to lead low towards the queen, hoping that West holds it. Here, West will rise with the king and you will score your queen later.

There is an old wives' tale regarding how you tackle a suit when you are missing the queen. It suggests that with eight cards between you, you should always finesse; holding nine cards, you should never finesse, but cash the ace and king and play for the queen to drop.

This isn't really correct.

The odds between finessing and playing for the drop are relatively close. If you have any information (from the bidding

– or lack of it) that leads you to believe that you know where the queen might lie, you should use that rather than blindly following the wives' advice.

e) If you have the slightest inkling that West holds the queen, finesse as opposed to cashing the ace and king.

f) If you suspect that East holds the queen, do not blindly finesse into his hand; instead, consider cashing ace and king and playing for the queen drop.

When you look at a suit combination, between your hand and dummy, sometimes you will realise that, if you tackle the suit, you will not make a trick – or sufficient tricks. At other times, you will conclude that a finesse is definitely wrong. In these situations, you must think about involving your opponents in the play of the suit in order to maximise your trick-taking potential.

2-way finesses and counting; Discovery play

If I had a penny for every time I begged my students not to take a 2-way finesse until the very end of the hand, I would be able to afford a very large bag of throat lozenges. Unfortunately, most inexperienced players see a possible finesse and take it immediately – and half the time they guess correctly.

a)   AQ94   b)   AJ5

      K1032   K106

a) If the opponents' cards split 3–2, all is easy but, if one holds four cards headed by the jack, it will be important to identify this before playing the suit. If East holds four to the jack, you can cash ace and queen and then lead through East, covering whatever card he plays. If West holds four cards to the jack, you can cash the ace, then the king and lead through West, trapping his jack between dummy's queen and nine.

b) The classic 2-way finesse missing the queen. If you know who holds the queen, you can either trap it between dummy's ace and jack, or between declarer's king and ten. All you have to do is to work out which opponent holds the queen.

     If you wait until the end of the hand, you give the opponents a chance to lead the suit for you – sorting out the position without any angst whatsoever. Failing that, you can remember the bidding, or lack of it, you can observe who throws away what (players guarding the queen of a suit tend not to throw away little cards), or even watch opponents' signals.

Let's take a look at a couple of examples:

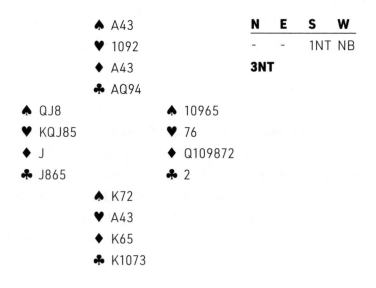

		N	E	S	W
		N	**E**	**S**	**W**
		-	-	1NT	NB
		3NT			

West leads K♥ and, despite a solid-looking combined 27pts, declarer can count only two spade tricks, one heart and two diamonds, so he will need all four clubs to make his nine tricks.

Most inexperienced players would win the second or third round of hearts and immediately attack clubs. Based on West holding five hearts and East only two, it is more likely that East holds length in clubs but, if you play for East to be long in clubs, you go down.

Let's see how we should play.

Since you have decided that you must make four club tricks, you must focus on that suit.

If the opponents club divide 3–2, all is easy but, if one of them holds four to the jack, you can still capture the jack and make your four tricks, but only if you know which opponent holds the length there.

You duck K♥ lead and, since you are not worried about West switching to another suit, you can duck Q♥ continuation too. When West plays a third heart, East discards a diamond, and you win with A♥. Now, before playing on the crucial suit, you need to make a "discovery play".

You cash A♠ and K♠ and note that West follows to the second round with J♠ or a crafty Q♠. You then cash A♦ and K♦ – and now, there is a revelation! West shows out on the second round of diamonds and, what's more, he throws away a heart!

This should convince you that West is guarding ♣Jxxx. If he held three or four little clubs, he would surely not have thrown away a winning heart, but instead a low club. If he had more than one winner in spades, he could afford to throw away a spade. It looks like he started with:

♠ QJx
♥ KQJxx
♦ x
♣ Jxxx

That is the only way his play makes any sense.

So, you play 3♣ to dummy's A♣, and then 4♣ to K♣ in hand. East shows out. Now, you know that West holds ♣Jx so, when you lead 10♣, if West plays low, so do you; if West covers with J♣, you win with Q♣, and dummy's 9♣ is a winner.

Thank goodness you didn't attack clubs immediately!

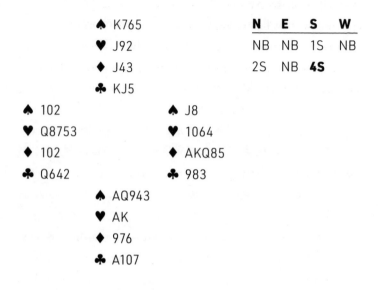

N	E	S	W
NB	NB	1S	NB
2S	NB	**4S**	

♠ K765
♥ J92
♦ J43
♣ KJ5

♠ 102
♥ Q8753
♦ 102
♣ Q642

♠ J8
♥ 1064
♦ AKQ85
♣ 983

♠ AQ943
♥ AK
♦ 976
♣ A107

When West decides to lead 10♦, declarer sees that he has three diamond losers, no trumps or hearts to lose, but a two-way finesse in clubs. Who holds Q♣? He must remember the auction and keep an eye on the cards played. Whatever else he does, he does not play on clubs until he has decided whom to play for the missing queen.

Declarer covers 10♦ with J♦, and loses the first three diamonds. East then plays 6♥, which South wins perforce. Declarer draws two round of trumps, East showing up with J♠. Now, South is almost certain that he knows who holds Q♣. How can this be?

East passed originally, yet he has shown up with ♦AKQ and J♠. That is 10pts. If he also held Q♣, that would give him

12pts and he would almost certainly have opened the bidding. Therefore, declarer places Q♣ with West. He leads 7♣ and, when West follows low, he finesses with dummy's J♣. When that holds the trick, he has no more losers and the contract is his.

Thinking is almost always better than guessing – it just takes a bit more effort.

a)	Q64		b)	K98	
A93		K1075	Q64		J732
	J82			A105	

c)	J108	
K92		Q764
	A53	

Frozen suits

a) The classic frozen suit. If you lead from either hand, you make no tricks. If your opponents lead it, you must score one trick.

b) If you lead, you make two tricks, always losing the third round to Q or J. If your opponents lead, the second hand to play plays low and you capture an honour. The other honour can now be finessed.

c) If you lead the suit, you make one trick; if your opponents lead it, you will likely make two tricks.

These examples illustrate why, as defenders, it is always dangerous to open up new suits – the vast majority of defence against suit contracts should be to find the safest lead at all times.

In each of these examples, to maximise your tricks, you must persuade your opponents to lead the suit. Usually, this will be achieved via an elimination endplay, where you play out all the safe suits with which an opponent could get off lead, and put them on lead when they can only lead the suit you want them to.

	♠ KQ86	
	♥ Q72	
	♦ 643	
	♣ A85	
♠ 72		♠ J9
♥ A1043		♥ K98
♦ J95		♦ Q1082
♣ QJ109		♣ 7632
	♠ A10543	
	♥ J65	
	♦ AK7	
	♣ K4	

South plays in 4S; West leads Q♣. Declarer faces one diamond loser and three heart losers – if she plays the heart suit herself. To succeed, she must force E/W to lead hearts. She plays like this: She wins trick 1 in hand with K♣, draws two rounds of trumps, cashes A♣ and ruffs dummy's last club in hand – eliminating the suit. Now, she cashes ♦AK and plays the third round. Whoever wins must play hearts or concede a ruff and discard. Now, declarer only loses two heart tricks and makes 4S.

Re-arrangement of finesses

Using your knowledge of the bidding, opening leads, and subsequent play, you may become convinced that a finesse is losing. You might attempt to force the opponent to lead away from the key honour, but sometimes you can re-arrange the finesse to give you an extra chance.

d)	A64		e)	QJ4	
Q83		10752	10962		K83
	KJ9			A75	

f)	AJ7	
K83		10654
	Q92	

d) From the bidding, you know that West holds the queen; there is no point in taking the standard finesse of playing low towards your KJ. Instead, lead jack from hand and, if West ducks, run it. West should cover, so you win with ace and now lead a low card towards your K9. If East plays low, insert 9, and you have made three tricks after all.

Leading the jack can never be correct if you do not hold either ten or nine.

e) The finesse is right but, when East covers the second honour – as she should – you do not hold 9 or 10 to make a third trick. Here, you must take the finesse, then hope that East chooses or is made to lead away from her king subsequently.

f) The finesse is right. You take it once, playing low to the jack; then hope that (or force) West to lead away from her king subsequently.

One key safety play

A Safety Play is a method of playing out a suit which best guards against bad distributions. There are many of these and, to be an expert player, you need to have an almost encyclopaedic memory of them.

The good news is that there is just one that occurs frequently – and it is well worth knowing. It is also nearly a perfect safety play, since it costs you nothing to use it almost always, but may well gain a whole trick for you when the cards are poorly distributed:

You hold eight cards in a suit between you and dummy, missing the queen and the jack.

Your goal is to accept that you will lose one trick, but avoid losing two tricks. How can you guard against one opponent holding: QJxx?

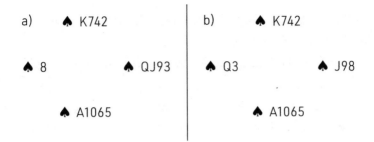

In these first two examples, you plan to cash the honour that is on its own first, and then lead low towards the honour with the ten.

So, you cash K♠ and lead 2♠. When East follows low, you insert the ten. If the suit is splitting badly – as in a) – your ten holds the trick and you lose only one trick to East's ♠QJ.

If the suit is dividing nicely – as in b), your ten loses to West's queen but, when you regain the lead and lay down A♠, East's J♠ falls and you still only lose one trick.

Please notice that, in a), it does not help East to rise with, say, the jack on the second round, since then you can win with A♠, return to dummy in a another suit, and lead towards your ♠106, avoiding losing more than one trick.

In all these examples, you cannot pick up QJxx if West holds them, because you need your honour and ten to surround the QJxx in order to avoid losing more than one trick.

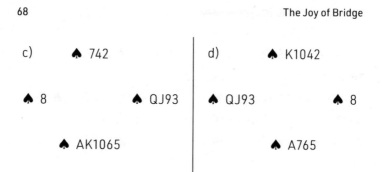

c)   ♠ 742   d)   ♠ K1042

♠ 8   ♠ QJ93   ♠ QJ93   ♠ 8

          ♠ AK1065   ♠ A765

c) A slightly different distribution for you, but the same procedure: cash A♠ first, cross to dummy in another suit, and lead 4♠ towards your ♠K10xx, inserting 10 if East correctly follows small.

d) You cannot succeed now if East holds the length because the honour and then ten is sitting over the West hand, so play for the possibility that West holds ♠QJxx. Cash A♠ first, then lead towards ♠K10x.

e)   ♠ K942

♠ ?   ♠ ?

          ♠ A1065

e) Now, either A10 or K9 can be used to guard against length in one opponent's hand, but which opponent? Perhaps the bidding will help you. In any case, as with all two-way finesses, if it can be left until the end – by which time, you may have gained key distributional information, it should be.

If you decide West is more likely to hold four spades, cash A♠ and lead towards dummy's ♠K9;

Whereas, if you feel that East probably holds length in spades, you would first cash K♠ and then lead from dummy towards your own hand, hoping to use your ♠A10 to make two tricks.

♠ ♥
♦ ♣

I'm about to tell you an innocent story about a private bridge class, the Wimbledon Championships, and an enormous German Shepherd dog and, suddenly, a not-so-innocent story pops into my head, told to a group of players competing in the International Pairs in London in the early nineties – a tournament I was lucky enough to administrate – by the inimitable Omar Sharif, himself a very fine bridge player.

Many years prior to this, he finds himself in the gilded gambling halls of Monte Carlo and, throughout the evening, he is aware of being scrutinised by a very beautiful but, he senses, slightly dangerous-looking lady with long dark hair, in a striking evening gown.

He resolves to find out more about her by inviting her for a glass of Champagne. He cashes in his chips at the cage, turns to face her, and she is gone.

Somewhat deflated, he returns to his suite, begins to remove his dinner suit and, just as this process is complete, from out of one of the ornate marquetry wardrobes, comes this lady. She is brandishing a pistol.

"Make love to me," she demands in an exotic European accent. "And, in the morning, I want to play bridge with you too."

Omar is shocked and fascinated but, he says, he is convinced that it is a real gun, and that she is really threatening him.

I recall this so clearly. He beckons the small group of late-night diners around the table, in the otherwise deserted dining room, to lean in towards him, and his magical, mischievous smile transforms his face.

"I am stark naked, I am in shock, and it took me almost two hours to convince her to put down the pistol – and it was real, and it was loaded. And, I have to tell you, I only have one lasting regret: we never did play bridge the next morning."

Anyway, back to the rather more parochial story I originally had in mind.

Many, many years ago, I taught four ladies of a certain age – all of whom had very distinct personalities. Our hostess was a hoot. She had the best laugh ever, but her false teeth always threatened to fall out. She also owned a German Shepherd puppy which, unlike all the many dogs she had owned in her lifetime, she had wholly failed to train.

The second lady was very proper, prim and erect, slim, tightly bound in beautiful clothes, but quite nervous. Even the most harmless tidbit of gossip was too much for her. The third lady was mad on tennis and, although not in her first flush of youth, played every single day, and the fourth lady was very serious, but also somewhat myopic, so she had to lean very low over the table to see the cards.

Although none would ever rise to the heights of a master bridge player, they were very dedicated and very keen so, despite it being a beautiful summer's day, with top matches on centre court at Wimbledon, we all assembled.

Imagine the scene if you will: a tasteful and charming garden flat off Putney Heath, fresh cut flowers in a vase, French windows open onto a sweet little garden, a tea-trolley with a cake and silver teapot. A beautiful antique card table with four exquisite armchairs and an embroidered stool for me. The dog sits quietly in the corner. A clock ticks melodiously, and chimes mellifluously on the quarter-hour.

It is a quintessential English bridge afternoon scene. Please hold that image in your mind. It is about unravel and ultimately implode in the most unusual fashion…

The hand is almost irrelevant but, by now, you may be craving some bridge, so here it is:

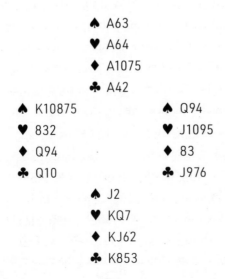

```
            ♠ A63
            ♥ A64
            ♦ A1075
            ♣ A42
♠ K10875              ♠ Q94
♥ 832                ♥ J1095
♦ Q94                ♦ 83
♣ Q10                ♣ J976
            ♠ J2
            ♥ KQ7
            ♦ KJ62
            ♣ K853
```

South plays in 3NT. West leads 7♠. Plan the play.

The correct line is as follows:

You assume that West has led from a 5-card spade suit, so you count it out. Five cards in the West hand; three in dummy; two in your own hand, so there are three in the East hand. Therefore, as you hold only one stopper in spades, you refuse to play your ace until the third round, by which time East has run out of spades.

You have one trick in spades, three in hearts, two in diamonds and two in clubs. That makes eight tricks. If you play on diamonds, you must score a ninth but, the secret is, having withheld your A♠ until East has none left, you can risk losing a trick to East, but not to West – because she holds two more spade winners.

So, you win trick 3 with A♥, get to hand with K♣, and lead a low diamond. When West follows low, you finesse with dummy's 10♦. As it happens, this holds the trick but, even if it had lost, it wouldn't matter, because East has no spades left to lead and you have control of every other suit. You cannot take the diamond finesse the other way around, as that would risk West winning, and West is the hand with the spade winners waiting to defeat you.

Anyway, that afternoon, the declarer does not make the contract.

This is why.

In the corner of the room, the television is silently relaying the action live from Centre Court. The tennis lady is facing the screen and, in the middle of this hand, there is a very exciting rally: lobs, drop shots, cross court attempted passes, and reflex volleys. The tennis lady 'ooohs' and 'aaaahs'. She is dummy, so this should really make little difference but for the fact that the German Shepherd wonders what the excitement is about. It snakes its way between its mistress's legs under the table. The prim lady feels her ankles being brushed against by a furry tail and exclaims. This excites the puppy further and, most unfortunately, it decides that this would be the perfect moment to stick its long, wet nose, up the skirt of the exclaiming lady.

I watch what unfolds as if it is slow motion. The myopic lady has her nose very close to the dummy. As the prim lady jumps up in shock, the table meets the nose of the thickly-spectacled lady, sending her bowling over backwards, the tennis lady stands but is also caught by the table, and over she goes too. The prim lady is screaming in a high-pitched tone, and trying to escape the dog, who has taken a fancy to what it perceives to be a splendid game. She, in turn, catches the tea trolley, sending it – at some velocity – towards our hostess. The prim lady and the dog make it to the hallway, and the trolley hits my hostess's chair, de-throning her too. The bridge table, and my set hand, is upended, and my hostess falls heavily, thankfully laughing away. Amidst this chaos, the dog re-enters the drawing room, proudly retrieves an item from the floor and runs into the garden triumphantly. As I rise – entirely unscathed physically, if not psychologically – to begin to help the ladies to their feet, I catch a glimpse of the dog's prize on the neatly mown lawn: its mistress's false teeth.

Little was learnt about the art of avoidance strategy that afternoon...

Avoidance

In all contracts, there are suits you would rather not have led by your opponents. The art of successful avoidance play is to identify which opponent is more dangerous to allow on lead and then find a method by which you can play the hand while avoiding letting that opponent on lead.

There are two classic situations:

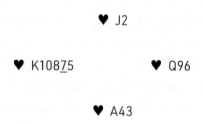

You play in 3NT and West leads 7♥. Assuming that the leader holds a 5-card suit, you count out the shape of the heart distribution and work out that East started with three hearts.

You refuse to win a heart trick until the third round, resulting in East now holding no more hearts and West holding two further heart winners.

Therefore, East is a safe opponent to allow to win a trick, and West must be avoided, since she holds two heart winners.

This is the other one:

♥ 92

♥ A108<u>7</u>4   ♥ J63

♥ KQ5

You play in 3NT and West, again, leads 7♥. You play 9♥ from dummy, East lays down J♥.

This trick reveals the layout of the suit. Assuming that West has led from a 5-card suit, East is marked with three hearts. She does not hold A♥ as, if she had, she would definitely have played it. She also does not hold 10♥ since, if she had, she would have played it rather than J♥.

Therefore, West started with ♥A1087x and East with ♥Jxx.

Nothing can be gained by ducking this trick, so you win with K♥. Which opponent offers the most threat now?

This is where some unthinking players go wrong. They assume that the hand with the longer holding is more dangerous, but look at the heart position now:

♥ 2

♥ A1084   ♥ 63

♥ Q5

If West gains the lead in another suit, your Q♥ is actually quite safe from attack. Either West leads A♥, and you make Q♥ later, or West leads another low heart and your queen makes immediately. The danger hand here is actually East because, if she gains the lead in another suit and leads back 6♥, your Q♥ is dead! If you play low, West wins with 8♥, lays down A♥ and takes her four winners; if you rise with Q♥, West wins with A♥ and takes four winners.

So, when both opponents still have the suit about which you are worried, it is usually the hand that can lead back, *through* whatever you have left, into the original leader's hand, who poses the most danger.

Once again, if West has led from only a 4-card suit, you do not have to worry: the opponents can only score three tricks, even if you let them back on lead again.

Let's take a look at a full deal.

West leads 7♥ again. Plan to play to ensure that you make your contract.

Dealer S	♠ K765		N	E	S	W
	♥ 92		-	-	1C	NB
	♦ K43		1S	NB	**3NT**	
	♣ A1072					
7 ♥ led		K♥ played				
	♠ A93					
	♥ AJ3					
	♦ AQ9					
	♣ KJ95					

West is assumed to hold a 5-card heart suit, so that places East with three hearts.

By playing K♥, East is denying Q♥, so it looks like West has led from ♥Q1087x.

What will you do at trick 1 – and subsequently?

The good news is that, on this deal, you could have picked either of the methods illustrated above.

You have 2 spade tricks, 1 heart trick and 3 diamond tricks. You only need three club tricks and you will definitely make those, even if you mis-guess who holds Q♣.

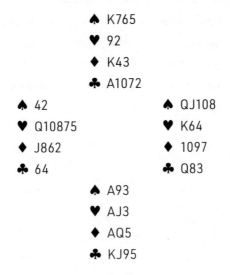

If you decide to hold-up your A♥ to exhaust East of her supply of hearts, you would duck two rounds of hearts and win the third. Assuming East now to be void in hearts, you would lead a low club from hand and, when West followed low, you would finesse with 10♣. Even if this loses (which, here, it does) it is only into the safe hand, East – who has no more hearts to lead.

Alternatively, you can win the first trick with A♥ and now realise that it is East who proffers the danger, having the power to lead a heart back *through* your remaining ♥J3 into the slavering jaws of West's ♥Q108x. Therefore, in order to avoid East ever gaining the lead, when you play clubs at trick 2, you should lead a low club to dummy's A♣ and then a low club back. When East follows with 8♣, you cover with 9♣ or J♣ and take the finesse. If it loses (which, here, it does not) West could not then continue leading hearts without giving you a further trick.

This hand was a bit special because you could choose either to win trick 1 or duck twice. This is because you could finesse the club suit in either direction. Often, what you do at trick 1 is determined by what options you have in the side suit you want to establish.

On the next two hands, South is in 3NT.

a)

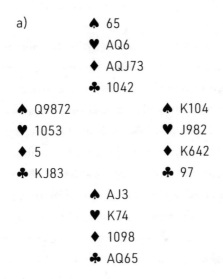

♠ 65
♥ AQ6
♦ AQJ73
♣ 1042

♠ Q9872
♥ 1053
♦ 5
♣ KJ83

♠ K104
♥ J982
♦ K642
♣ 97

♠ AJ3
♥ K74
♦ 1098
♣ AQ65

West leads 7♠. Do you win trick 1, or plan to duck twice?

b)

♠ 65
♥ AK62
♦ AQ7
♣ J1082

♠ Q9872
♥ 105
♦ J1064
♣ K9

♠ K104
♥ J983
♦ K93
♣ 74

♠ AJ3
♥ Q74
♦ 852
♣ AQ653

Again, West leads 7♠. Do you win trick 1, or plan to duck twice?

On hand a) your route to success will involve setting up the diamond suit. If West has K♦, you will always successfully finesse it, but if East holds it, he will always win it.

Therefore, you must plan to exhaust East of his supply of spades by refusing to win A♠ until East has none left. You duck the first two spade tricks and win the third perforce. Now, you can attack diamonds and, when East does win K♦, he has no more spades to lead, and you have control of every other suit.

On hand b) your route to success will involve setting up the club suit. If East has K♣, you will always successfully finesse it, but if West holds it, he will always win it.

Therefore, you must plan to protect your spade holding by beating East's K♠ at trick 1 with A♠, crossing to dummy with a top heart and then leading J♣, running it when East plays low. West does win K♣, but he cannot lead a further spade without your J♠ scoring a trick either immediately or in the second round.

There is one last form of avoidance which occurs occasionally and which, if you can master, will boost your ability to control the hand.

When I was learning bridge, this was a technique that convinced me that this was the game for me. It is so simple and logical yet, without being shown an example, almost impossible to work out. I hope that it inspires you too.

In this version, you cannot keep a dangerous opponent off lead, but you might be able to strand the safe opponent on lead – and, so, the same effect is achieved in a different way.

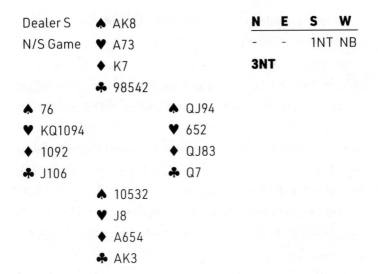

Dealer S   ♠ AK8
N/S Game   ♥ A73
              ♦ K7
              ♣ 98542

N	E	S	W
-	-	1NT	NB
3NT			

♠ 76   ♠ QJ94
♥ KQ1094   ♥ 652
♦ 1092   ♦ QJ83
♣ J106   ♣ Q7

              ♠ 10532
              ♥ J8
              ♦ A654
              ♣ AK3

West leads K♥. Declarer counts two spade tricks, a heart, and two diamonds. He needs four more tricks and, as long as the club suit behaves, those tricks can come from dummy's long suit. However, once declarer has ducked two rounds of hearts and won the third round, West will hold two heart winners. How can declarer keep West off lead?

In simple terms, he can't but, if East holds Q♣, he can arrange to strand East on lead with that card.

Here is how declarer should play.

Assuming that West started with five hearts, declarer counts East for three.

He ducks the first heart and, when West continues with Q♥, declarer ducks this also. Winning the third heart, he starts attacking clubs. He leads 2♣ from dummy and, when East plays low, declarer must win to avoid West from winning and cashing his two heart winners.

Next, a spade is played to dummy's K♠ and a second low club is led. East produces Q♣ and declarer... plays low from hand! This strands East on lead with the top club and, when South regains the lead, A♣ can be cashed, and dummy reached via K♦ to enjoy the two remaining club winners.

Had East not produced Q♣ on the second round, South would have to win and lay down a third club, hoping that East had started with three clubs to the queen.

If East rises with Q♣ on the first round of the suit, declarer ducks that. As long as East holds Q♣, or three clubs, declarer can strand him on lead.

The key here is to lead from dummy *through* the East hand, so that declarer can choose to win or duck once he's seen what card East has played.

If you followed along to these deals, nodding your head because you feel this is simple, that is great. But, if like most social bridge players, you found these quite tough concepts, I urge you to re-read this section and even to lay out these deals, using real cards, on a table.

I say this because, once you have mastered the art of standard avoidance plays, you will never think them hard again, and it will open your mind to thinking more deeply about your opponents and the threats they pose to your wellbeing...

Not drawing trumps

Back to suit contracts again now – and how about this for an aphorism?

"Many a man lives under the arches of Waterloo Bridge because they didn't draw trumps quickly enough."

This is, I'm afraid, another old wives' tale.

I know many glamorous and delightful old wives, but they know me well enough not to spout this kind of nonsense. Most of the folks who lose their pennies at rubber bridge do so because they draw trumps too quickly.

a) ♠ Q1065
    ♥ 82
    ♦ AJ73
    ♣ K42

    ♠ AKJ73
    ♥ K754
    ♦ 2
    ♣ A65

In 4S, you receive Q♣ lead. Do you draw trumps, or not?

If you do, you go down.

West holds A♥, so you will lose two hearts and the third round of clubs. You therefore need either to ruff three diamonds in your own hand, or two hearts in dummy. The latter is less stressful, but give E/W a chance to lead spades and, seeing your plan, they will. On their own, they can only take out two rounds, leaving you with two in dummy, but if you've already drawn a round or two for safety, you'll find yourself at least one trump short.

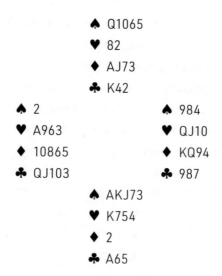

What about here?

You play in 4S. West leads 10♥.

You try playing low from dummy, but East wins with Q♥, cashes A♥ and switches to 8♣.

You still have a diamond loser, so what do you do now?

Win, and draw trumps?

If you do, you go down (again).

East's 8♣ looks like it is from top of rubbish (it would be very silly to lead away from Q♣ with J♣ to your right), so West probably holds Q♣. Your only hope lies in setting up a diamond winner on which you can discard your losing 10♣. To do that, you will need entries into the hand which contains the long suit you are trying to establish. You have three: A♦, and ♠KQ. You will need them all.

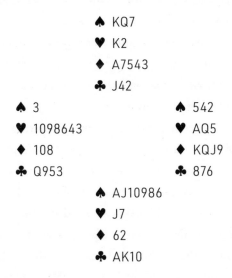

Win trick 3 with A♣ and play 2♦, ducking in dummy (you will need A♦ when it is useful to you). East should win and lead a second club. You rise with K♣ and now lead 6♦ to A♦, and then a low diamond which you trump in hand. West shows out. You cross to dummy's Q♠ and play a fourth diamond and ruff again in your hand. This has pulled all East's diamonds and set up your fifth diamond as a winner. In case trumps break badly (they do) lay down A♠ next and, finally cross to dummy with a spade to K♠. Now, you play 7♦ and discard your 10♣.

Beautifully played.

Notice that, had you played even one round of trumps prematurely, East could have led a trump when he won the first diamond trick and one crucial entry to dummy would have been blown.

If you need extra tricks from ruffing, or to set up dummy's long suit, hesitate before drawing trumps.

If you found that suit-establishment play easy, that's wonderful but, if you didn't, I urge you right now to grab a pack of cards, lay out the hand on a table and play it through, as described, several times, until it all seems obvious.

Once you've mastered that play, it will transform your confidence and ability as a declarer.

When I suggest laying out a hand at home and playing it through, please do. It really makes a huge difference.

All my teaching life, on hands like the one above, I've said to students: if that's not completely clear, it really will be worth your while getting a pack of cards, laying them out on a table, and playing the hand through until it seems obvious.

Almost no one ever does.

Then, a few years back, I had a breakthrough:

A student of mine who had always struggled with card-play had a hand like the one above to play in a class. She played it perfectly. I was super-impressed.

"I did what you suggested after last week's class," she told me, within earshot of other students.

"I laid out all the set hands we played in your class on my bridge table at home, and played them all several times. Suddenly, it clicked."

I repeated her testimony to the whole class. Everyone nodded sagely. They, too, were amazed that after so long this student had finally mastered a suit establishment play.

I entreated everyone to do the same this week.

Next week, none of my students made their prepared hands and, upon enquiry, I learnt that not one of them had laid out the previous week's hands at home on a table and played them through until it all seems obvious.

Not only that, but there was no sign of my newly enlightened student.

A few weeks later, she was still absent from my classes. When I caught up with her at a bridge club, I told her:

"I'm missing you."

"I know what I'm doing now," she told me firmly. "I don't need lessons anymore."

It's a simple story, prosaic even:

Teacher finally enlightens student and loses student forever. The end.

Remembering the auction; Counting

In previous hands, we have already seen examples of counting.

You can count both distribution and points, and you will be helped in your detective work if you can recall the auction, including everybody's passes.

Look at this deal:

	♠ K1085		**N**	**E**	**S**	**W**
	♥ AJ62		-	-	NB	NB
	♦ AK		1H	NB	1S	NB
	♣ 1042		3S	NB	**4S**	
♠ J7		♠ 62				
♥ 543		♥ Q98				
♦ 10872		♦ QJ543				
♣ AKQJ		♣ 987				
	♠ AQ943					
	♥ K107					
	♦ 96					
	♣ 653					

West leads A♣. Declarer faces three clubs losers and a search for Q♥. If she can identify which opponent holds that card, she can finesse it successfully. If West holds it, she can trap Q♥ between dummy's A♥ and J♥; if East holds it, it can be gobbled up between declarer's K♥ and 10♥.

But, how can declarer discover its location?

*Facing a two-way finesse, always delay taking
it until the last possible moment.*

Here, West leads A♣, K♣, and Q♣, and then gets off lead safely with 8♦. Declarer draw trumps, and thinks about what she knows.

West has ♣AKQ and has shown up with J♠. That is 10pts. If she also held Q♥, she would have had 12pts.

Let's recall the auction. South dealt and passes, and then West passed also. If she had held 12pts, would she not have opened the bidding?

On this basis of a negative inference (West passed originally), declarer can place Q♥ with East. She leads a diamond to dummy's other top honour, and then 2♥. When East follows low, she finesses with 10♥ and this holds the trick.

I love the detective part of bridge. One private lesson, a student arrived late, so I played a couple of hands with the other three – and this was one of them:

	♠ AJ7	
	♥ 862	
	♦ 9653	
	♣ A103	

N	E	S	W
-	-	-	NB
NB	NB	**1NT**	

♠ 652		♠ 10843
♥ AQJ43		♥ K5
♦ A7		♦ J1082
♣ Q54		♣ 976

	♠ KQ9	
	♥ 1097	
	♦ KQ4	
	♣ KJ82	

West led Q♥, East overtook with K♥ and returned 5♥. Having taken five heart tricks, on which East threw two spades and 6♣, West got off lead with 6♠. I won this in dummy and led a diamond to my K♦, losing to West's A♦. Another spade was led and I won, completely confident I knew who held Q♣. I even announced all this at the table to demonstrate how counting at bridge often solved the mystery of where missing cards lay.

"Since West has shown up with ♥AQJ and A♦, and she passed originally, you," I told East, "hold Q♣."

"Play it out," East said, maintaining a poker face. So, I did.

I crossed to A♣ and led 3♣. When East played low, I finessed with J♣ and West took a card out of her hand to play. Then, she bent down and retrieved a card from the floor. She counted the cards in her hand and giggled:

"I've been playing with 12 cards all along."

And, with that, she snapped the Q♣ on top of my J♣, and said proudly.

"That fooled you. One down!"

Assuming, then, that your opponents know what they hold in their hands (in my experience, far from an automatic assumption), you can gain quite a bit from recalling the auction and watching which cards opponents play.

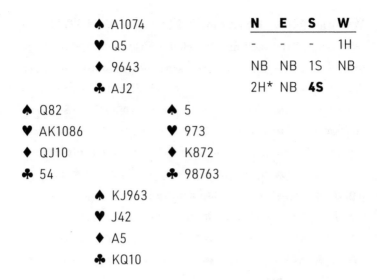

North's 2H was an Unassuming Cue-bid indicating 11pts or more, with at least 3-card support.

West led A♥ and K♥ and she then switched to Q♦.

Declarer holds two heart losers and a diamond loser, and she is worried about Q♠.

Holding nine cards in a suit, headed by ace-king-jack, with no information about your opponents' cards, you might just cash the ace and king and hope that the queen fell. That would not work here.

> *When the opponents have bid, always add up how many*
> *points you hold between your hand and dummy, and*
> *calculate how many this leaves for your opponents.*

You count that your side holds 25pts, leaving 15pts for the opposition. When, at trick 3, West led Q♦, that denied holding K♦, so you place East with that card. That leaves only 12pts for West, who opened the bidding. Therefore, West holds Q♠ and you should finesse her for it. This thinking brings home the contract.

	♠ AJ10		**N**	**E**	**S**	**W**
	♥ KJ43		-	-	1NT	NB
	♦ AK4		4NT*NB		**6NT**	
	♣ A54					

	♠ 9			♠ Q86542
	♥ 97			♥ 1062
	♦ J9853			♦ 107
	♣ QJ1076			♣ 98

	♠ K73
	♥ AQ85
	♦ Q62
	♣ K32

North's 4NT response is a Quantitative Raise (see page 235). South accepted the invitation and bid 6NT.

West led Q♣, and declarer counts her tricks:

2 in spades; 4 hearts, 3 diamonds and 2 clubs. 11 tricks.

There is only one possible way to score a twelfth trick and that is to make an extra spade trick. If declarer knows where Q♠ is located, she can finesse that opponent for it and make her slam.

There is no bidding to help her place that card, so how does she discover its location?

*Facing a two-way finesse, always delay taking
it until the last possible moment.*

Yes, you have seen that italicised sentence before but I repeat it because no one ever listens to me. Do everything else before deciding on that finesse.

So, here we go then.

At trick 1, duck the lead. You can't possibly make a third club trick, so lose the trick you have to lose early on. This will help you to fathom out the shape of your opponents' hands.

West will continue with J♣. This you win and cash your other top club. When you do this, East shows out, so now you register that this means that West started with five clubs.

Next, you play out all your diamonds. On the final round, East shows out again, so you can place five diamonds in the West hand. That is ten of West's cards accounted for.

Now, you play out all your hearts: West follows to two rounds and shows out on the third. So, what do we know?

West started with five clubs, five diamonds and two hearts. That leaves her with just one spade.

Declarer can now play 3♠ to dummy's A♠, noting that West produces 9♠. Then, she leads J♠ and, when East plays small – as she should – declarer also plays low from her hand too. She *knows* that West is now void and that the finesse will work.

West is void, the finesse does work and the slam is brought home.

Obviously, if all that is too much work, you can just guess who holds Q♠ – but, for me, that isn't much fun.

One last one for you to try yourself:

<pre>
              ♠ Q1032   N   E   S   W
              ♥ A42   NB   NB   1S   NB
              ♦ J64   3S   NB   4S
              ♣ K65

10♦ led
              ♠ AK974
              ♥ KJ6
              ♦ 532
              ♣ A3
</pre>

You have three diamonds to lose and Q♥ to deal with. Who holds it, and what can you do about it?

East wins trick 1 with Q♦, and cashes A♦ and K♦, before switching to 2♣. You win in hand with A♣ and draw two rounds of trumps required. Who has Q♥?

You don't know yet. You need to keep playing. You play 3♣ to dummy's K♣ and ruff 6♣ in hand. You are doing this not to create a trick, but to see what happens on the third round of clubs. And, something does happen. East shows up with J♣.

If you have been watching, you will have observed East play ♦AKQ. On the second round of trumps, she dropped J♠ and, now, on the third round of trumps, J♣. That is 11pts. She didn't open the bidding when she had the chance, so she won't also hold Q♥ – that would give her 13pts.

So, West has Q♥, but what can you do about it?

Whatever you do, don't lead J♥ from your hand. West will just cover that with Q♥, you will win with A♥, but you will lose the third round of the suit.

Your only hope here is that West's Q♥ is a singleton or doubleton.

You lay down A♥ and K♥ and, when you see West's Q♥ fall, you are permitted a small smile of satisfaction.

		♠ Q1032			**N**	**E**	**S**	**W**
		♥ A42			NB	NB	1S	NB
		♦ J64			3S	NB	**4S**	
		♣ K65						
♠ 65				♠ J8				
♥ Q9				♥ 108753				
♦ 10987				♦ AKQ				
♣ Q10874				♣ J92				
		♠ AK974						
		♥ KJ6						
		♦ 532						
		♣ A3						

All our counting has been about finding a missing queen. That is the most common use for it, but there are many other occasions when you can place an ace or king in a hand and that will help you to play your hand more effectively. There are occasions when you are counting distribution, that you can discover that one opponent definitely holds a missing queen or jack; that an opponent holds much greater length in a suit than his partner, assisting you in your chosen line of play.

This all takes effort, concentration, and the ability to add up to thirteen. We can all manage that and, if we find we can't, it's time for a little bit of mental training.

Train your brain

I read a wonderful book about training your memory by a chap who was world memory champion. He could recall the sequence of up to two packs of playing cards just by flicking through them and using his brilliant techniques. Great book, improved my memory enormously: I can't remember the title or the author's name, but it was Dominic-something, I think.

We don't need to remember a sequence of a hundred-plus cards, just to be able to add up to thirteen and keep an eye on cards played. Trying to remember the cards gone and, ideally, who played them and in what order, is less a matter of memory and more down to trying to concentrate and immerse yourself in the world of 52 cards, but I do have a simple brain-training exercise for you.

Whenever you have a few moments free, lay your hands on a deck of cards, shuffle them, and then turn the top card face up, and then turn it over. Do this with the first five cards. Then, return to them and try to remember which card came out first, second, etc., turning them over to confirm that you are right.

You may find that, at first, you struggle even with just five but, slowly, your brain will make you concentrate on those cards and five will become easy. Then, increase the number. I got to thirteen and called it a day but, even if you manage only seven or eight over a period of days or even weeks, that'll be just fine.

The purpose of this is not simply to boost your concentration skills, but also to persuade you to look at cards played and remember them, almost subconsciously. After doing this, you will find that you naturally retain much more information about the cards played and from where they emanated.

Play out all your trumps

I have been recommending this play for 40 years; every time I play, I realise that if my opponents had done this, they would have either given themselves a chance to make the hand, or would definitely have succeeded. Yet, so often, players just don't!

Let's be clear: if you don't need the trumps for trumping anything, and you can't use them as entries to set up a long suit, then they are your plaything and you can use them as you wish. You face a seemingly unavoidable loser. This is the time to play them all out. And, quite often, it is the final trump – the one you'd really rather not part with – that causes the opponents the problem.

What you are aiming to achieve here is to pressure your opponent (or sometimes both opponents) into throwing away something they would rather hang on to. They may do this because they are genuinely squeezed – whatever they throw would be wrong – or they may think that they're squeezed – so they throw what they think they can throw, but it turns out to be wrong or, finally, they're just not paying much attention, are irritated that you are playing out all your trumps, so they throw away whatever is closest to their thumb.

Here's a pretty example:

			N	E	S	W
E/W Game	♠ 10864		-	-	-	1S
Dealer W	♥ J54					
	♦ K105		NB	NB	3C	Dbl
	♣ 653		NB	3H	4C	4H
♠ AKQJ7		♠ 93	**5C**	NB	NB	**Dbl**
♥ KQ3		♥ 109862				
♦ QJ86		♦ 9743				
♣ 2		♣ 108				
	♠ 52					
	♥ A7					
	♦ A2					
	♣ AKQJ974					

South's jump to 3C showed a strong hand, with about 8 playing tricks, or 18pts or more.

West's double is for take-out; his raise from 3H to 4H, having made East bid, was an overbid, but he probably hoped that his partner held five hearts to the ace and nothing more and that ten tricks might just roll in. Perhaps because West bid 4H so confidently, North decided that 4H sounded like it would make and so, knowing that his partner would hold a 7-card club suit to bid twice, he decided to take the sacrifice in 5C. In fact, 4H doubled (if it could have been) would have failed by two tricks (if South gets his diamond ruff), and that would score N/S +500.

Anyway, 5C is now the contract and West led A♠, K♠ and Q♠ which South trumped. Trumps could be drawn in two rounds, but there appears to be an unavoidable heart loser. How can declarer possibly not lose 7♥?

With no use for the trumps in dummy as an entry, or to be used for ruffing, this is the moment to run off all the trumps.

Focus on the West hand. He must hang on to J♠, as this card stops dummy's 10♠ from becoming a winner. West must also protect ♦QJxx to prevent declarer from playing A♦, K♦ and using 10♦ to discard 7♥ from hand. And, just to add to his agony, he has to protect his hearts to stop dummy's J♥ from becoming a winner.

Let's just use the correct terminology here. West is squeezed in three suits and there are two cards in dummy which aren't winning now but threaten to become winners: 10♠ and J♥. These cards are called "menaces". These wouldn't be worth anything if there wasn't a means of access to enjoy them should they become winners, and this is why declarer leaves K♦ safely in the dummy so he can get there later.

Finally, it is worth noting that squeezes usually work (even if you don't know that they are working) when one opponent has all the high cards. That way, they have too many responsibilities with which to cope. For example, if East held Q♥, West could throw away all his hearts and East could prevent dummy's J♥ from becoming a winner.

Here, the auction has told us that West has a big hand with cards in every suit apart from clubs.

So, here we go:

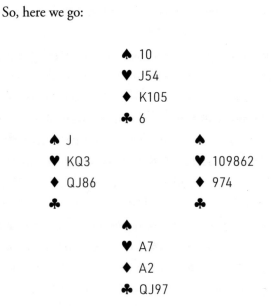

South has trumped the third round of spades in hand and led ♣AK.

Now, he continues to play his trumps.

On the next round, West can safely throw 6♦.

On the next round, West can discard 3♥.

On the next round, West can... Er... Nothing. West is right royally squeezed.

If he throws J♠, dummy's 10♠ is now a winner on which declarer can discard 7♥.

If he throws Q♥, declarer can lay down A♥, felling West's K♥, and dummy's J♥ is a winner.

If he throws 8♦, declarer can play A♦, K♦ – felling West's ♦QJ and dummy's 10♦ is a winner.

The key is that you do not need to know that this is happening, you merely need to play off your trumps (in this case, you don't even need to play your final one) and watch what West plays, hanging onto whichever suit(s) West throws away, and discarding any suit West hangs on to.

If this all goes well, you will hear West sigh heavily, and witness a look of painful constipation transform your opponent's previously confident (smug?) features into a mask of agony.

In this example, West could not throw any card that would save him. But, sometimes, if only your opponent knew, he could afford to throw something away but, not knowing what, he throws the wrong thing.

N/S Game	♠ 96			**N**	**E**	**S**	**W**
Dealer S	♥ 854			-	-	1H	1S
	♦ K743			2H	3S	**4H**	
	♣ A862						

♠ AKJ74		♠ Q1052
♥ 103		♥ 62
♦ QJ10		♦ 8652
♣ J93		♣ KQ10

	♠ 83
	♥ AKQJ97
	♦ A9
	♣ 754

South doesn't really want to bid 4H, but 3S might easily have been making (in fact, it's one or two down) and 4H can't actually make but, as you'll see, it will.

West leads A♠ and K♠ and then switches to a trump (a club works much better, but it's not obvious that it's the correct suit to attack). Declarer wins and faces two inevitable club losers.

Does he give up?

No. He runs off five trumps…

This time, let's look at East.

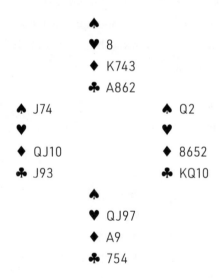

South has lost ♠AK and played ♥AK. Now, he plays three more trumps.

East can safely throw his 2♠ and Q♠ but on the fifth trump, what should he discard?

If he throws 10♣, he might just give away the contract if South started with ♣J54.

So, he throws 2♦ – and that is a disaster!

Declarer now plays A♦, 9♦ to dummy's K♦, and ruffs 3♦ in hand with his final trump. Because East threw away his fourth diamond, the fourth diamond in dummy is now a winner. Declarer gets there by leading a club to dummy's A♣, and he throws a losing club from hand on the winning diamond.

East was not squeezed. He thought he was and that he couldn't afford to throw away a club but, because West actually held ♣Jxx, East could have thrown away a club, hung on to his four diamonds, and defeated the contract.

This play then has the technical name of "Pseudo Squeeze".

Again, you don't need to know that this is happening and you certainly don't need to know what it's called: you just play off your trumps and hope that something good happens.

The number of times I have done this and made an extra trick I can't tell you. Sometimes, I know exactly what is going on, and at other times, I have no idea. But, all these plays have one thing in common: you can look very clever at the end whatever happens. I am quite good at looking clever. In fact, I'm much better at looking clever than being clever. And I'll let you into a secret. Looking clever is not about being clever: it's about denying being clever, but modestly claiming that you got lucky, or it was hard for your opponents to know what to do. If you can sympathise with your opponents, they'll be very impressed indeed.

A school friend of mine was a very keen amateur magician. He performed brilliantly even if, technically, you sometimes spotted how he did it.

"What," I asked him one day, "do you do when a trick goes wrong?"

"It's very simple," he told me. "No one ever knows that the trick has gone wrong, because you don't tell the audience what you're going to do in advance. That way, if you were planning on making a white rabbit appear and suddenly you can't, you can make the ace of spades pop up behind someone's ear, and everyone still thinks you're magic."

Remember this story when you don't know what to do, so you play out all your trumps (or, occasionally in no-trumps, your long suit). Your opponents don't know what the trick is – you may very well not know what the trick is – but you flamboyantly play out all your cards and, at the end, hope that the trick goes well. Even if it doesn't, you've put on a show and, at the very least, your partner will appreciate it.

By the way, on that last hand, East mis-defended. It wasn't easy for him at all and, on other layouts, he might have done the correct thing, but a really good pair wouldn't have made that mistake.

Keeping secrets

There are many ways of obtaining information at the bridge table but, when playing against less experienced players, one of the easiest it to take all the free information they proffer.

We have already discussed this situation:

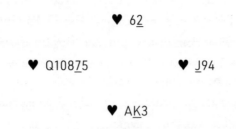

In a NT contract, holding both ace and king, win with the king.

If you just held the king, say ♥K43, you would have to win now, in case West had led from AQ987 and, if you duck, East would return a heart and you would lose the first five heart tricks.

Whereas, if you held only ♥A43, you would certainly duck the first trick and, probably, the second one also.

So, winning with the ace almost certainly reveals that you also hold the king, whereas if you win with the king, East is unsure who holds the ace.

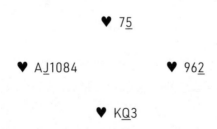

There may be times when it is correct to duck the first trick here but, usually, to win will be the correct action. Here, you want to win with the queen.

East knows that you hold the queen, because West's lead of J♥ obviously denies Q♥, but he does not know who holds K♥. West should know that, on his lead of an honour, East should play any honour he has immediately – but not everyone knows that, or remembers to do it, so it might sow some doubt in his mind.

> *When winning a lead in a no-trump contract as declarer, win with a card the leader has already denied holding. This will almost always be the lower of touching honours from your hand.*

Conversely, in suit contracts, it is usually correct to win with the higher of two touching honours.

Look at this first trick when South is playing in, say, a 4H contract:

♣ 97<u>4</u>

♣ Q86<u>3</u>   ♣ J1<u>02</u>

♣ <u>A</u>K5

West leads 3♣ and East plays the lower(est) of her touching honours.

East knows that West does not hold the ace, since she would not lead away from it, and West knows that East doesn't hold the ace as, if she did, she would play it at trick 1.

Therefore, South must win with the ace. It is a card she is known to hold and playing it gives away no additional information.

Generally, in suit contracts, the declarer should win with a card the leader (and, possibly, his partner) has already denied holding. Usually, this will be with higher(est) of touching cards.

Largely, these policies are the opposite to the way that defenders would play since, in their case, they are trying to help their partner place missing cards, whereas the declarer need not be honest with his partner, since he is dummy, and probably thinking about a large gin and tonic, how to – politely – select the biggest slice of cake, or how unlucky he is to have you as a partner!

Playing the card you are known to hold is an excellent play at all times, since it gives away nothing, and often provides an opponent with a losing option. Here, in defence, we see a classic example:

Declarer could be in either a suit or a no-trump contract, wanting to make all four club tricks here. Look how easy it is for him:

♣ AJ7

♣ Q106   ♣ 854

♣ K932

Declarer leads 2♣ (West plays 6♣) to J♣ and this holds the trick. He cashes dummy's A♣ and West drops his 10♣. Now, declarer leads 7♣ from dummy and, when East follows, he knows that West has Q♣, so he plays his K♣ and West's Q♣ drops.

Easy, eh?

But, try this: Declarer plays 2♣ (West plays 6♣) to J♣ and this holds the trick. Both West and the declarer know that West holds Q♣. Now that J♣ has been played both West's Q♣ and his 10♣ are the same value. When declarer cashes dummy's A♣, West drops the card he is known to hold: Q♣. Now, declarer leads 7♣ from dummy and, when East follows, he has no idea who holds 10♣ – because West hasn't told him – and so, what does he do? If it were me, I would finesse now with 9♣ and lose to West's 10♣. Only three tricks and a poor result for me.

This play of dropping the card whose position is already known is second-nature to good bridge players but anathema to those less experienced. So, when an expert drops the queen, you have no idea where the ten might be but, when an average player drops the queen, you can be pretty certain that it is his only remaining card. Unless, that it, he has understood and applied this example.

Try to play cards you are known to hold and retain cards about which the declarer currently has no knowledge.

Getting your opponents to help you

If the opposition is pretty inexperienced, and they haven't read the section on defence, they will probably help you anyway: most defenders shove tricks down the throats of grateful declarers. However, better players will have to be persuaded, nay forced, to help you against their will. Sometimes, this is your only hope of success.

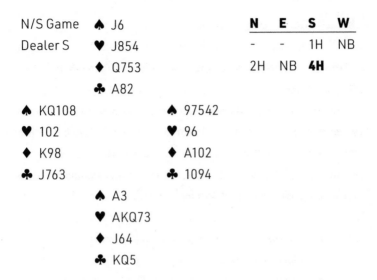

N/S Game
Dealer S

♠ J6
♥ J854
♦ Q753
♣ A82

♠ KQ108
♥ 102
♦ K98
♣ J763

♠ 97542
♥ 96
♦ A102
♣ 1094

♠ A3
♥ AKQ73
♦ J64
♣ KQ5

N	E	S	W
-	-	1H	NB
2H	NB	**4H**	

South alights in 4♥ and West leads K♠. Declarer is downhearted. She has a spade to lose and three diamonds, since the latter holding is a frozen suit. If she leads a diamond, she will almost certainly lose all three tricks but, if she can persuade either East or West to start leading them, she will only lose two tricks.

How might declarer arrange that?

It's not going to be a matter of persuasion. No defender seeing that dummy is willingly going to lead a diamond: they must be compelled!

Declarer wins the lead immediately and draws two rounds of trumps; she plays out all her clubs; she gets off lead by playing a spade.

Look at the situation: with no cards in dummy or her hand in either black suit, if West leads a club or a spade, declarer can trump in dummy and discard a diamond from her own hand. This is called giving a "ruff and discard".

This is usually very beneficial to the declarer and should be avoided 99.9% of the time. Here, it means that South can get rid of one of her diamond losers and restrict her losers in the suit to just two.

Look closely: this is why declarer played off all her clubs before losing the lead. If she hadn't, West could have led a club and that wouldn't have helped the declarer at all. This process of playing out all the cards in a suit, leaving none in either hand, is called "elimination" or "stripping".

> *As a defender, you should strive to avoid leading a suit*
> *in which you know – or strongly suspect – that both*
> *dummy and the declarer are void. Doing so provides*
> *declarer with a chance to trump in one hand and*
> *discard a loser from the other: a big advantage.*
> *Avoid giving declarer a ruff and discard.*

Of course, West does have one alternative option: to lead a diamond – exactly what South wants. Imagine West leads 8♦. Dummy plays low and East must play A♦ to avoid South scoring her J♦. East is similarly embarrassed: a black suit lead would again provide a ruff and discard, so she returns a diamond. Holding both Q♦ and J♦ and with only K♦ outstanding, declarer can only lose one more trick and, again, her contract is secured.

This type of advanced declarer play is called an "Elimination Endplay". Declarer sets up the hand so that all suits that would be safe for a defender to lead are eliminated, or stripped out, and then she gets off lead, normally towards the end of the play, embarrassing the opponent.

Let's look at a slightly more difficult example:

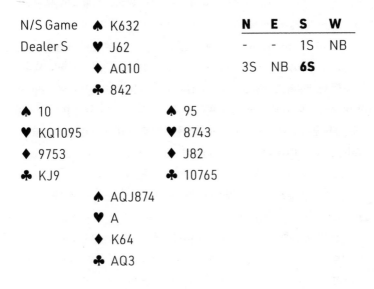

N/S Game   ♠ K632
Dealer S   ♥ J62
             ♦ AQ10
             ♣ 842

♠ 10   ♠ 95
♥ KQ1095   ♥ 8743
♦ 9753   ♦ J82
♣ KJ9   ♣ 10765

             ♠ AQJ874
             ♥ A
             ♦ K64
             ♣ AQ3

N	E	S	W
-	-	1S	NB
3S	NB	**6S**	

South punts the slam and faces K♥ lead. She has no losers in spades, hearts or diamonds, but two losers in clubs. She may lose Q♣ to K♣, and she will definitely lose the third round of clubs.

You can see that the club finesse fails and, with it, surely, the contract.

But, if declarer can persuade West to lead a club, all will be well. However, West will have to be compelled to do so, since there is no way in the world that West will willingly lead a club around to your strong holding…

Let's set up the position. West's lead guarantees that he also holds Q♥. That is good news. At the appropriate moment, when we can make leading anything else either impossible or equally unappealing, we can throw West back on lead.

We win trick 1 perforce, and draw two rounds of trumps. Now, we eliminate the safe suits that West could lead when we out him back on lead.

Play 4♦ to dummy's Q♦, and then lead 6♥ and trump it in your own hand. This is very important. If we don't do this, West could lead a heart and that wouldn't help us at all. Now, we play K♦ and 6♦ to dummy's A♦.

Here comes the clever bit: we lead J♥ and, instead of trumping it in our own hand, we throw away our certain club loser: 3♣. If West doesn't win with Q♥, we have made our contract but, of course, West does. But, now, look at the situation West faces.

If West leads a red suit, because you are void in both dummy and your own hand, you can trump in dummy and throw away Q♣ from your hand – a ruff and discard.

If West tries a club, you take both tricks with your ♣AQ.

Finally, to get your endplay juices flowing, here is an example in 3NT.

Game All	♠ AKQJ		**N**	**E**	**S**	**W**
Dealer W	♥ QJ43		-	-	-	1D
	♦ 9		Dbl	NB	2NT	NB
	♣ A872		**3NT**			

♠ 1063		♠ 952
♥ K9		♥ 10876
♦ KQJ1074		♦ 82
♣ QJ		♣ 10963

	♠ 874
	♥ A52
	♦ A653
	♣ K54

West leads K♦. You have four spade tricks, one heart, one diamond and two clubs. You need only one more trick but, since you have only one stopper in diamonds, if you let West back on lead, he will make five diamond tricks, plus whatever other trick you lose to him.

You have 28pts between you, but West opened the bidding, so we can place all the outstanding points with him, and that means that the heart finesse will lose. Can you find a way of making West lead a heart around to you, allowing you to score both, say, Q♥ and your own A♥?

Your only hope, apart from the very slim chance that West holds a singleton K♥, is to throw West on lead when he only has diamonds and hearts left. Let's play together.

You duck the first two rounds of diamonds noting, on the third round, that East shows out. This marks West with six diamonds. Now, we will play out all four spades, discarding 4♣ from hand on the final one – and, again, observing that West throws Q♣ on the last spade. Now, we cash A♣ and K♣ – and, crucially, on the second club, we see West discard 4♦.

Why would West throw away a winner in his long suit? To protect his ♥Kx.

With no black cards in his hand, we know that West holds only two diamond winners and ♥Kx. Thus, we get off lead with our last diamond. West wins and cashes a further diamond winner but, then, he is stuck on lead at trick 12, with nothing but ♥K9 from which to play. Whichever card he plays, you will win both the last hearts and record nine tricks.

In a no-trump contract, having eliminated the other suits, the card you often get off lead with is one in the suit the opponent led originally. He will cash a winner – or winners – there, but must then lead the one other suit he has left.

I have enjoyed bridge all over the world, from the card room in the roof of the famed Gotham Hotel in Manhattan, to the refined surroundings of the Hong Kong Club. I have bid and played high in the Alps and frequently aboard trains. I have shown bridge problems at 36,000 feet and in the loose mushroom aisle of the local supermarket. I have played bridge with two intoxicated teammates in Amsterdam and two far-too-sober teammates in the USA. I have never played in the

Channel Tunnel, but I did take part in a hand underwater – and a truly bizarre scenario it was.

Before embarking on a stint at the National Theatre in London, I took a trip around the world. I was twenty years old and, as well as bridge and golf and tennis, I wanted to scuba dive. Having visited friends in Hong Kong and Australia, I flew to the second largest island of Fiji and, following lengthy travel involving light aircraft, speedboats and an ancient Land Rover, arrived in a resort deserted but for me, the dive team, and one middle-aged American couple. On rather small horses, we rode, idyllically, along the beach – the photographs testify that my feet were barely a foot from the ground – we took dinner under palm trees. The couple were a husband-and-wife gynae-cological team – they saw their patients together – and keen bridge players. On discovering that I shared one of their areas of expertise, they outlined their plan for their last day. Using the lead-weighted playing cards they had packed – this *really* is a true story – we would enact an underwater hand of bridge. A Fijian diving instructor would ignorantly sit as dummy but then we could rightfully claim to have played amongst the fishes.

All went well: the lagoon boasted no current; we found a flat rock; thirteen thick "cards" were handed to each of us; the pre-ordained contract 3NT. This is, more or less, what it looked like:

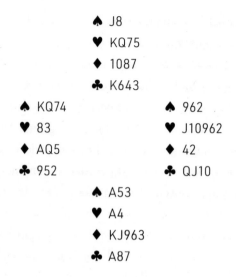

```
                    ♠ J8
                    ♥ KQ75
                    ♦ 1087
                    ♣ K643
        ♠ KQ74                      ♠ 962
        ♥ 83                        ♥ J10962
        ♦ AQ5                       ♦ 42
        ♣ 952                       ♣ QJ10
                    ♠ A53
                    ♥ A4
                    ♦ KJ963
                    ♣ A87
```

The lady gynaecologist was South and her husband East. The contract was 3NT and I led 4♠. Declarer rose – in watery slow-motion – with J♠ from dummy, which won. The trick was gathered together, a stone laid on top the four "cards" in front of her. She led 7♦ and ran it. I won with Q♦ and led K♠ which was allowed to win. A third spade followed, taken by declarer's A♠ and now my A♦ was forced out. I cashed my last spade and followed suit patiently as declarer made the rest.

Photographs recorded this extremely rare event but, despite leaving my details, they were never forwarded to me.

Over a sunny cocktail, we reviewed the hand.

"I set it all up," she announced, "so that you guys could defeat me in 3NT, but Paul led the wrong card."

Exhilarated and sun-kissed as I was, I disputed her criticism.

"If you lead K♠," she pronounced, "I never score dummy's J♠."

I shook my head. "That's not what I had."

"You had ♠KQ1074."

I denied it and, unrepentant, she showed me the jotting from which she had set the hand.

"I never had 10♠."

She checked through the still salt-sticky deck. There was no 10♠ to be seen.

Somewhere, on the house reef of the island of Vanua Levu is a, by now barnacled, lead-weighted 10♠. Whenever it appears in my hand, I stare at that card accusingly.

To spoil a (hopefully) good story with analysis, just look at the spade layout of that hand the way it was intended to be:

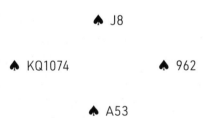

$$\spadesuit \ J8$$

$$\spadesuit \ KQ1074 \qquad\qquad \spadesuit \ 962$$

$$\spadesuit \ A53$$

If you incorrectly lead fourth highest from West's spade holding – 7♠ – declarer should play J♠ from dummy and it holds the trick.

If you correctly lead top of a broken sequence from two touching honours and the next card but one, you can often smother that missing card.

Here, you lead K♠, your partner can indicate how many cards he holds by using a simple count signal – see page 153 – and, when declarer ducks – as she will – you can continue with Q♠, rendering dummy's J♠ useless and only conceding one trick, as opposed to two. If you regain the lead, as I did here, you will cash four spade tricks plus the one with which you gain the lead.

This is why top-of-sequence and top of a broken sequence leads are so important, both against suit contracts and No-trump contract. Get these right and you will save many tricks, breaking contracts that would otherwise have made. Go a little further, and combine them with a count and jettison understanding and you will break open the joys of good defence.

Defensive Essentials and Techniques

Unless you are a very lucky card holder, you will find yourself defending half the time. Yet, often, players talk for hours about bidding ideas, and spend mere seconds on defence agreements.

In this section, I suggest some simple, highly effective signalling and discarding methods which, while you should not assume every stranger will understand, are fairly standard and designed to help you work out the important stuff.

And, as in the declarer section, there are ideas which will benefit you as an individual although, hopefully, partners will be on the same wavelength.

Let's start with what I think is the most important piece of thinking there is when defending a suit contract.

The three prongs of defence thinking
This is how you should be thinking whenever you are defending a suit contract.

Declarer has three ways of making extra tricks; which he adopts usually depends on the shape of dummy. Occasionally, if the declarer's hand is very distributional, or the hand is being played "upside down", dummy isn't as important but, on the vast majority of occasions, dummy will determine the declarer's plan.

If dummy is balanced, declarer cannot easily trump losers, or set up a long suit, so will have to rely on finesses or, more commonly, defensive errors.

If dummy contains a shortage, declarer's plan is likely to involve trumping losers in dummy.

If dummy contains a long suit (this may be as few as 4-cards, but more commonly, 5 or 6-cards), declarer's plan will be to draw the trumps, set up the long suit, and discard his losers from hand on those cards.

In defence, you must seek to identify the declarer's likely plan – and then base your defence on countering that plan.

Ideally, you would do this from listening to the bidding, anticipating the look of dummy, and getting underway from the opening lead. However, once you see the dummy hand on the table, there is no excuse not to base your decisions on this basis.

When dummy hits baize, take your time to try to assess what plan the declarer may have.

If you see that dummy is balanced

Take no risks in defence. Lead as safely as possible at all times. Lead top-of-sequence.

Lead a suit that will make declarer trump in his own hand (or whichever trump holding is longer).

Lead trumps.

Do not open up new suits, lead away from honour cards, cash winners unless you have the card below also.

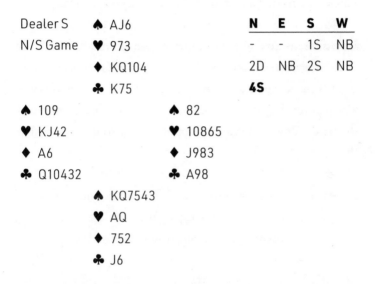

Dealer S	♠ AJ6		N	E	S	W
N/S Game	♥ 973		-	-	1S	NB
	♦ KQ104		2D	NB	2S	NB
	♣ K75		**4S**			

```
♠ 109                    ♠ 82
♥ KJ42                   ♥ 10865
♦ A6                     ♦ J983
♣ Q10432                 ♣ A98

              ♠ KQ7543
              ♥ AQ
              ♦ 752
              ♣ J6
```

South ends in 4S and, with A♦, A♣ and Q♣ all badly placed for him, and dummy's diamonds unable to produce more than two tricks, the contract cannot be made UNLESS West defends in a way that is not safe.

If West leads 3♣, at any time, declarer can play low from dummy and force East to win with his A♣ – this reduces declarer's losers to just one in clubs.

If West leads a heart, that gives declarer a free finesse and allows him to make his contract.

Defenders should NEVER lead dummy's long suit.

Only a trump lead is safe here. Dummy is balanced and the declarer's plans will fail. When West wins A♦, he must lead another trump or another diamond; when West wins K♥, he must lead another trump or another heart. He must never broach a new suit leading away from an honour.

East is safe to lead a trump or a heart, but nothing else.

If possible, avoid making speculative leads from Qxxx or Kxxx, and especially from Jxxx.

Whenever you lead away from an honour, you are allowing a card lower than that honour to win (or contribute strongly to) the trick. Why promote your opponents' cards into better than they are?

It is particularly dangerous to lead from an honour card when the one beneath it is to your right, since you are then making that card as important as the one from which you have led:

a)	Q63	b)	J32	c)	Q8
	K872		Q84		K1043
	AJ4		A105		A2

a) If you lead 2, you allow South to run this to Q in dummy and then finesse you for your K, catching it between AJ for three tricks. If you refuse to lead this suit, declarer cannot make more than two tricks.

b) If you lead 4 here, declarer makes two tricks. If you refuse to play your Q until dummy plays J, declarer only makes one trick.

c) If you lead 3, declarer can play low and win with Q – and ends up losing no trick.

To lead away from an honour when you know the strength in on your left is far less dangerous since this is a finesse which the declarer may well be able to take anyway. For example:

♠ A72   If North opened 1C, South bid 1H and North
♥ 43   jumped to 4H, you would know that the strength
♦ K743   lay in North's hand and that South could be quite
♣ J852   weak. If you were on lead with this hand, it would
           be quite safe to lead 3♦, even 2♠(!), since you
would be leading through strength and up to weakness – a safe scenario. By the way, 3♦ is recommended here unless you feel very frisky.

If you see that dummy contains a shortage
Lead trumps to cut down how often declarer can ruff his losers in dummy.

Lead a trump from 2 or 3-card holdings. Generally, do not lead trumps with a singleton (you might spoil your partner's strong holding there), or from a 4-card holding (it is better to lead a long suit and try to force declarer to trump in his own hand), or from a likely, natural, trump trick, such as:

Kx or Qxx, or Jxxx.

Keep leading trumps at every opportunity.

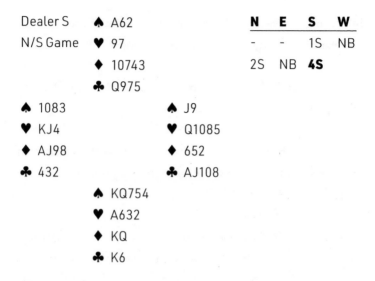

N	E	S	W
-	-	1S	NB
2S	NB	**4S**	

Whenever your opponents bid only one suit, unless you have an ace-king sequence, or a weak hand with a singleton, your default lead should be a trump. This is because the bidding reveals that there is unlikely to be, threatening suit in dummy, nor a completely balanced hand. Therefore, the most likely scenario is that dummy may contain a shortage, a feature the declarer wishes to exploit to ruff losers from his hand.

On the hand above, if West leads 3♠ and, when he regains the lead in hearts, leads a second trump, declarer can only trump one heart loser in dummy, so goes on to lose two hearts, A♦ and A♣. Any other lead gives him time to follow his plan and make his contract.

If dummy contains a long, threatening suit

Lead unbid suits aggressively and hurry to take your tricks there. If you don't, declarer will draw trumps, and discard all his losers on the long suit.

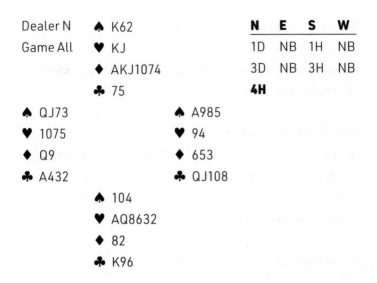

Dealer N	♠ K62		N	E	S	W
Game All	♥ KJ		1D	NB	1H	NB
	♦ AKJ1074		3D	NB	3H	NB
	♣ 75		**4H**			

Here, the bidding announces, loud and clear, that North holds a high-quality 6-card diamond suit, and South has a 6-card heart suit. If West ignores this information and makes a safe lead of a trump, declarer will draw trumps, run through six diamond winners, throwing black-suit losers away from hand, and make two overtricks.

If, instead, West leads one of the two un-bid suits, say Q♠, East-West should make two spade tricks. When East wins on the first or second round of spades, he must switch to the other unbid suit – clubs, leading Q♣. This results in East-West taking the first four tricks and defeating the contract.

See how silly leading a trump would be on this auction?

So, please be thinking like this when defending suit contracts:

Balanced dummy: lead as safely as possible at all times. Let your high cards beat your opponents' cards.

Dummy containing shortage: lead trumps

Dummy containing long suit: lead unbid suits aggressively, to take tricks quickly.

Leading shortages

Whenever you lead a short suit – a singleton or doubleton – you are often leading into declarer's strength and length. Before leading a short suit, always consider how likely it is that you will be able to receive a ruff, or ruffs.

For example:

West		N	E	S	W
♠ QJ8		1D	NB	1S	NB
♥ 4		3S	NB	**4S**	
♦ AJ75					
♣ KQ963					

This would be a terrible time to lead your singleton heart. Your opponents have bid game, for which you expect them to hold about 26pts. You have 13pts, so your partner has one or two at most. He won't hold A♥ and he won't get on lead to return a heart to you.

If you want a heart ruff, you're more likely to get it by hoping that declarer tries to play on the suit before drawing trumps.

But, even then, do you want a heart ruff? You have a natural trump trick anyway, and that is more likely to cause declarer problems than ruffing a heart.

Lead K♣ instead. This is a much more sensible lead.

Whereas:

West	N	E	S	W
♠ 852	1D	NB	1S	NB
♥ 4	3S	NB	**4S**	
♦ J752				
♣ J9863				

Now, your partner is likely to hold at least 10pts and your trump holding is useless. If you are really lucky, partner will hold A♥ and A♣ and you can defeat the contract with two aces and two ruffs.

Lead your singleton 4♥ now.

*Lead a shortage only when holding a weak
hand, and two or three small trumps.*

This is even more true when leading a doubleton, which can be a very dangerous lead. You are exposing your partner to an immediate finesse and often playing around into the strong hand. Occasionally, a doubleton lead works perfectly, and everyone is very pleased with themselves. More often, such a lead gives away tricks to the declarer, and sometimes gives away the contract. Then, everyone keeps very quiet and hopes no one has noticed!

*Lead a doubleton only if partner has bid the suit,
or you are extra weak with three little trumps.*

What would you lead here?

West	**N**	**E**	**S**	**W**
♠ QJ98	1C	NB	1H	NB
♥ J64	2H	NB	**4H**	
♦ AJ752				
♣ 9				

Q♠ is the correct lead. 9♣ is a terrible lead, because it is leading dummy's long suit, and that is exactly what declarer will want to do.

In defence, never lead dummy's long suit.

Never – and that includes when you are considering leading dummy's longest suit, that may only be four cards in length. Just don't do it! Try, as hard as possible to lead something else.

When you hold four trumps, it is very rarely correct to lead a shortage. Instead, you should seek to make the declarer ruff in the hand with the long trump holding. Imagine if declarer holds five trumps and you make him ruff in his own hand: he is now down to four trumps – he can't draw all your trumps without running out himself and, that, will be a major blow to him.

> *With four trumps, lead your (or your side's) longest suit to try to make declarer trump in his own hand and shorten his trump holding. This is called a 'Forcing defence'.*

This can even work when declarer has six trumps.

			N	E	S	W
Dealer N	♠ AJ6		NB	NB	1H	NB
Love All	♥ Q8		1NT	NB	3H	NB
	♦ Q643		**4H**			
	♣ 8752					

```
Dealer N      ♠ AJ6              N    E    S    W
Love All      ♥ Q8             NB   NB   1H   NB
              ♦ Q643           1NT  NB   3H   NB
              ♣ 8752           4H
♠ 93                  ♠ 108742
♥ K652                ♥ 4
♦ J1098               ♦ AK75
♣ A93                 ♣ 1064
              ♠ KQ5
              ♥ AJ10973
              ♦ 2
              ♣ KQJ
```

Compare West's modest trump holding with South's strong suit. How can West bully declarer?

Holding four trumps, you should lead something that might make declarer trump in his own hand. Your long suit is diamonds and you hold a lovely sequence, so lead J♦.

Declarer only has three losers: K♥, A♣ and a diamond, but watch the effect of the forcing defence:

Declarer plays low from dummy and J♦ holds the trick. West leads 10♦ and, again, declarer plays low and so does East. South trumps. He is now down to five trumps.

South plays 5♠ to dummy's J♠ and lays down Q♥. When East plays low, so does declarer, and West ducks. Declarer continues with 8♥ and is a bit nonplussed when East shows out, but he plays 9♥ from his hand and West wins with K♥.

What does West do now?

He leads another diamond. When East plays K♦, South has to trump, and now declarer is down to only two trumps, just like West. If South draws both trumps, when he then loses A♣, West will lead a fourth diamond and East's A♦ will win. 4H is one off.

If declarer doesn't draw the trumps, when West wins A♣, he leads his fourth diamond, East plays A♦ and declarer will trump. But, now, South only holds one trump; West still has two. West scores another trump trick and, again, South is defeated.

So, when declarer trumps in the hand that is long in trumps, don't be put off from continuing to lead that suit, quite the contrary: keep making him do that. It cannot create any extra tricks for declarer, but it can seriously shorten his trump holding perhaps, like in the hand above, causing him to lose control of the trump suit and the hand!

Play the correct card to inform partner

This is an incredibly simple tip but one which is heartfelt, because students and social players often fail to do this.

I remember chatting about quite advanced bidding ideas for hours with a friend of mine and, then, on the first hand of a duplicate evening, he played the wrong card. Not only did it throw the defence in that suit but, because he had denied a particular card which I then placed in the declarer's hand, I got absolutely everything wrong. From that moment on, I wasn't sure what any card my partner played meant.

So, please remember that:

> *When your partner leads to you, try to win with*
> *the lower, or lowest, of touching cards.*

I led 3♦, partner held ♦KQxx, and incorrectly played K♦ – that denies the queen.

If you correctly try to win with Q♦, and declarer wins with A♦, partner knows there is a good chance that you also held K♦.

So, remember this:

You lead from the top of a sequence and receive the lead (from partner or opponents) by playing the bottom of sequences.

When leading	When receiving the lead
KQJ8	KQJ8
QJ9	QJ9
AK32	AK32
10984	10984
7642 (top of rubbish)	7642

What card do you lead in the suit your partner has bid?

Unless you have a really good alternative, lead the suit your partner has bid.

This may well be the correct lead but, almost as importantly, if it isn't, you have kept your partner happy – a greatly underestimated tactic for success at the bridge table.

If you make speculative leads, refusing to lead your partner's suit, every time they go wrong, fissures will appear in your partnership. Mistrust will breed and then nothing will work as it should.

When you lead your partner's suit, except in rare circumstances, you should follow the standard rules:

Top-of-a-sequence: from any two touching honours, lead the top honour.

Three or four low cards: lead either your highest card, or M.U.D. (Middle, Up, Down: the middle card, the higher, then the lowest card).

Three or four cards to an honour: lead your lowest card.

Doubleton: always the higher card.

Many older players believe that you should always lead the highest card in your partner's suit, but this is not correct, and frequently gives away tricks and contracts. There are a few times when leading the highest card is the best action: when partner has made a lead-directing double; when the opposing hand through which you will be leading is much stronger than the opposing hand that will play fourth.

These are, however, rarities, and the rules above will see you right the vast majority of the time.

One very diligent student in a large class wanted me to repeat those rules, so I did.

Despite the promise of notes, she was scribbling away in her notepad:

"What do lead from four cards headed by an honour?" she asked me.

"The lowest."

"And from three cards headed by an honour?"

"The lowest."

"And from a doubleton?"

"The higher."

"And with a singleton?"

I paused a moment, attempting to work out whether she was joking. She was not. She looked up from her pad, her pen poised. She stared at me over her reading glasses. There was murmuring from the cheap seats.

I'll leave you to work that one out.

When **not** to lead your partner's suit

This is a thinking woman's game: no rule is inviolate. There are definitely times when leading your partner's suit is the wrong way to go.

West		N	E	S	W
♠ 6		1C	1S	2NT	NB
♥ J874		**3NT**			
♦ QJ1095					
♣ A63					

Here, to lead a spade is lazy. South has clearly shown two stoppers in spades (and a good 10–12pts) and, holding a singleton, having led it, you won't be able to again. Instead, to lead Q♦ looks rock solid. If partner holds either A♦ or K♦, she should play that card immediately and return your suit. You continue leading diamonds until the opposition's stopper is dislodged and then, when you gain the lead with A♣, you can cash your winners.

Even if partner does not hold a top diamond honour, your side may well have chances to lead diamonds three times and then, again, 3NT is defeated.

You may experience an interaction such as one I had:

Partner: "Why didn't you lead my suit?"

Me (confused): "We defeated the contract."

Partner: "But why didn't you trust me?"

Me (realising that partner is obviously very needy): "I do trust you, but if I had led your suit, they would have made their contract."

Partner: "It's still very dispiriting…"

Me: (silence: there's no pleasing some partners…)

Leads against NT contracts

Providing that it has not been bid, you generally lead your longest suit.

You then follow the standard lead system:

If that suit contains no card higher than the ten, lead the top, or second-highest card:

Top-of-Rubbish: 97532; 108652; 65432; 10432

Notice that, when you hold the ten, that card may be a trick-taking asset, so usually you opt for the second highest card, otherwise you lead the top card.

If the suit is headed by an honour, or non-touching honours, lead the fourth highest card:

Fourth Highest: K97<u>5</u>3; Q106<u>4</u>; KJ9<u>6</u>2; AJ8<u>3</u>

The lead of a low card promises an honour, or broken honours, at the head of your suit. Your partner should try to win the trick and return your suit.

If the suit you have chosen to lead is headed by three honours (the ten is an honour only when it is accompanied by friends, like the jack or the nine), you must lead top of the sequence of touching honour cards, or top of a broken sequence of honour cards:

Top-of-a-Sequence: <u>K</u>QJ53; <u>Q</u>J106; <u>J</u>10932; <u>10</u>9853

Any touching cards that start with cards lower than the ten are not counted as sequences; you should treat them as all low cards and just lead top-of-rubbish.

For example, 876 is not a sequence in bridge, it is just the start of my phone number.

If you hold a suit headed by AQ10, this is three honours and, technically, you should lead either the ace or the queen (depending upon whether you hold an outside entry). However, since this can lead to confusion, I recommend that all but the most experienced players opt to lead fourth highest from this combination:

AQ10<u>6</u>3; AQ10<u>5</u>

If you hold two touching honours and then the next but one, this is called a Broken Sequence. It is a big advantage to you to lead the top card from this holding, since it ensures that if either the declarer or the dummy holds a singleton or doubleton of the missing card, it is nullified immediately and, should they hold three cards including the missing card, it can often swallowed up by either you or your partner.

Let me show you:

Dealer S	♠ AJ6		**N**	**E**	**S**	**W**
N/S Game	♥ J6		-	-	1NT	NB
	♦ KQ3		**3NT**			
	♣ Q6542					

♠ 932		♠ Q1084
♥ KQ1074		♥ 952
♦ 1098		♦ 75
♣ K3		♣ A1087

	♠ K75
	♥ A83
	♦ AJ642
	♣ J9

If you incorrectly lead 7♥, declarer should rise with J♥ in dummy. This holds the trick and, together with five diamond tricks, ♠AK and A♥, 3NT is made.

If, instead, you correctly lead top-of-a-broken sequence: K♥, dummy's J♥ never makes. You continue leading top hearts until A♥ comes out, and now declarer cannot make more than 8 tricks.

Top-of-a-Broken Sequence: KQ1063; QJ97; J10842; 109762

There is one last variation on the top-of-sequence theme, and that is:

Top-of-an-Interior Sequence: AJ1053; KJ108; AQJ64; Q1098

These leads tell partner that you hold three significant cards, stop opponents' lower cards from making tricks, and distinguishes between a suit you would like your partner to win and return from a top-of-rubbish lead.

With one major exception, all these leads are the same against suit contracts, and they all offer a big advantage over simply leading fourth highest. The major exception is this:

Against a suit contract, never lead away from a suit headed by an ace

Do not lead an ace unless you also hold the king

If your partner has called the suit, you might choose to break these rules, especially holding a doubleton ace, but otherwise remain wary – it is a very dangerous lead.

So, AJ1053; AQ106; AJ83; A10987; A54 are all NOT leadable against a suit contract.

Pick a different suit.

♠ ♥
♦ ♣

I played in a pro-celebrity bridge match in a smart hotel in London a few years back. I was partnered with a distinguished actor, Hilton McRae, whom you will have seen on stage at the RSC and on television in all sorts of dramas. I'm not entirely sure how he got himself roped into such an event, because his bridge was fairly basic, and he was absolutely terrified. There were many England and international players involved and a good number of spectators.

I told my partner that I was unshockable (at the bridge table), and I really didn't care how we did, as long as we enjoyed ourselves. Much to his relief, no one was watching our table.

The first few hands passed with a revoke, an unexpected pass and some nervy card play, but we soon settled into our own rhythm.

We plodded along mid-table most of the tournament. We made rank amateur mistakes and expert misjudgements, but we also bid and made a dramatic grand slam. About three-quarters of the way through, something very odd happened. Slowly but surely, more and more spectators came to our table. Soon, they were surrounding us. Was it because we were playing the best bridge?

Not at all! It was because we were smiling and laughing and enjoying bridge for the – exceptionally challenging – game that it is. We showed the spectators our cards and asked their advice; we quietly complimented each other when we did something right.

Experts at the other tables started shushing us, and we just laughed. The more we enjoyed ourselves, the better we did. We ended up finishing far higher than we had any right to expect.

I got a right telling off from some of the older famous experts.

I was convinced then – and I remain of the view today – that they got it all wrong. The event was designed to promote bridge:

not expert bridge, or bridge brilliance, but the game itself. And far too many people just can't seem to enjoy their bridge anymore. Bridge is an utter joy, played at any standard, with friends, or competitively. My role has always been to convince others of this.

The morals to be derived are simple:

Put your partner at ease; smile, laugh.

Enjoy bridge for what it is – a game.

Don't conflate wanting to win and taking it seriously (I always do) with not enjoying yourself. You can, and should, do both.

The more you are enjoying yourselves, the better you will do.

Overtaking and jettison
Against a NT contract if partner leads top-of-a-sequence, you must play any honour immediately.

This understanding simplifies so many things, I am always amazed when people do not know it/do not play it. There are very rare times when doing something different may have a slight advantage, but do not worry about these.

Remember that, when your partner leads an honour against a no-trump contract, it is from one of the following holdings:

Top-of-a-sequence: KQJ, QJ10, etc – three touching cards
or
Top-of-a-broken sequence: KQ10, QJ9, J108
or
Top-of-an-interior sequence: AJ10; K1098

When he leads from these holdings, he is desperate to know where the missing honours are located or if you as his partner, hold no honour, how many cards you have in the suit.

So, when partner leads an honour against an NT contract, you will almost always play any honour you have immediately. If you fail to play an honour, you will be denying holding it (except on very rare occasions, which we will examine in a moment).

South is the declarer in 3NT. West, your partner, leads. You are East.

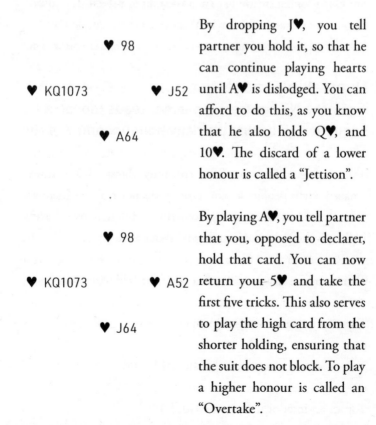

By dropping J♥, you tell partner you hold it, so that he can continue playing hearts until A♥ is dislodged. You can afford to do this, as you know that he also holds Q♥, and 10♥. The discard of a lower honour is called a "Jettison".

By playing A♥, you tell partner that you, opposed to declarer, hold that card. You can now return your 5♥ and take the first five tricks. This also serves to play the high card from the shorter holding, ensuring that the suit does not block. To play a higher honour is called an "Overtake".

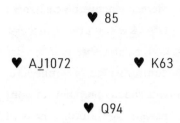

♥ 85

♥ AJ1072   ♥ K63

♥ Q94

By overtaking with K♥, you win the trick, and you can return 6♥. This catches declarer's Q♥ between your partner's ♥A10 and allows your side to take the first five tricks.

It should go without saying that this is used for all four suits but, just in case you thought it only applied to hearts, here's an example featuring a different suit. West leads K♣.

♣ 98

♣ KQ1073   ♣ 852

♣ AJ4

You play 2♣. Declarer correctly plays 4♣. Your failure to play either A♣ or J♣ confirms that you hold neither and that the declarer holds both. Your partner now knows not to continue playing clubs but, instead, to try a different suit.

The two – very rare – occasions when you would not play an honour in these situations are:

When you think you hold more cards in the suit than your partner, or when, by playing an honour, you set up a trick for the dummy that would not normally be scored:

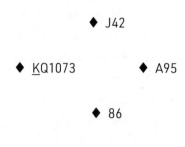

♦ J42

♦ <u>K</u>Q1073   ♦ A95

♦ 86

Here, if you overtake partner's K♦ lead with your A♦ and return 9♦, you set up dummy's J♦ as a winner. So, you should play low. If your partner is thinking, he will deduce that, if the declarer held A♦, he would have won the trick, knowing that J♦ would be a second stopper. Therefore, declarer doesn't hold A♦ and you do. Partner should then continue with a low diamond to your ace and you return your final diamond to take the first five tricks.

If you don't hold an honour card, you show Count – how many cards you hold in the suit, allowing partner to deduce the declarer's holding and, hopefully, make the correct decision whether to continue leading that suit, or to switch to a better line of attack.

For all the details and examples of showing count, see page 152.

Interpret the meaning of your partner's lead

Here is a simple problem that many players got wrong. What would you do?

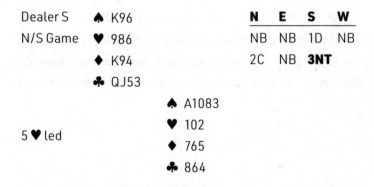

		N	E	S	W
Dealer S	♠ K96				
N/S Game	♥ 986	NB	NB	1D	NB
	♦ K94	2C	NB	**3NT**	
	♣ QJ53				
	♠ A1083				
5♥ led	♥ 102				
	♦ 765				
	♣ 864				

Your opponents reach 3NT quickly and partner leads 5♥.

Dummy follows low and you play your 10♥, taken by declarer's Q♥.

Declarer leads 3♦ to dummy's K♦, and then plays Q♣, running it to your partner, who wins with K♣.

Partner now leads 7♠, dummy plays 6♠.

What do you do, and why?

The key to your decision will be interpreting partner's 7♠ lead. What is it?

As you can see all the other cards higher than this except for Q♠ and J♠, and partner would never lead low from ♠QJ7, his 7♠ must be top of rubbish.

Why is he leading this now?

The only explanation is that he feels that he cannot lead another heart (his original lead) himself, and he is trying to get you on lead to play a heart back to him.

Therefore, you must win, and shoot back 2♥.

If you do that, you will defeat the contract by two tricks.

If you play low to force out a spade honour from South, declarer makes nine tricks: 1 spade, 1 heart, 4 diamonds and 3 clubs.

```
       Dealer S      ♠ K96
       N/S Game      ♥ 986
                     ♦ K94
                     ♣ QJ53
   ♠ 754                        ♠ A10832
   ♥ AJ753                      ♥ 102
   ♦ J102                       ♦ 765
   ♣ K2                         ♣ 864
                     ♠ QJ
                     ♥ KQ4
                     ♦ AQ83
                     ♣ A1097
```

When your partner leads a second suit in a defence: if he plays a low card, he wants you to win and return that suit; If he leads a high card, he wants you to win and return his original suit.

Throughout the defence, the lead of a low card suggests interest in that suit and a desire for you to win and return it;

The lead of a high card suggests lack of interest in that suit and a desire for you to win and return a different suit.

Whereas:

			N	E	S	W
Dealer S	♠ K96		NB	NB	2NT	NB
N/S Game	♥ 864		**3NT**			
	♦ 1094					
	♣ QJ53					
5 ♥ led		♠ 10832				
		♥ 102				
		♦ A75				
		♣ 864				

Your opponents reach 3NT quickly and partner leads 5♥.

Dummy follows low and you play your 10♥, taken by declarer's Q♥.

Declarer leads J♠ to dummy's K♠, and then plays Q♣, running it to your partner, who wins with K♣.

Partner now leads 2♦, dummy plays 4♦, and you win with A♦.

What do you do, and why?

This time, partner has led his lowest diamond, indicating interest in that suit. If he had wanted you to return a heart, he would have led a high diamond. His choice of his lowest diamond asks you to win and return that suit. So, you correctly return 7♦ and, as a result, your side takes four diamond tricks, as well as partner's K♣ and you defeat the contract.

```
Dealer S      ♠ K96
N/S Game      ♥ 864
              ♦ 1094
              ♣ QJ53
♠ 75                          ♠ 108432
♥ K9753                       ♥ 102
♦ KJ62                        ♦ A75
♣ K2                          ♣ 864
              ♠ AQJ
              ♥ AQJ
              ♦ Q83
              ♣ A1097
```

Pressure in defence

In this next set of tips, let's look at dealing with pressure in defence…

Let's start with a common defensive problem:

			N	E	S	W
Dealer S	♠ 64		-	-	**4S**	
E/W Game	♥ AQ853					
	♦ Q4					
	♣ J862					

♠ 932	♠ 10
♥ J6	♥ K102
♦ AKJ96	♦ 107532
♣ A105	♣ Q743

♠ AKQJ875
♥ 974
♦ 8
♣ K9

Let me show you what happens if East and West are lazy.

South opens an aggressive pre-empt and is left to play there.

West leads A♦, K♦ and South ruffs. Now, being a good declarer, here come at least five more trumps. At the table, East felt that he must protect clubs so, having thrown away three diamonds, he then pitched the seemingly irrelevant 2♥. Now, South led 4♥ and finessed with Q♥, losing to East's K♥. East led back a low club, which South ducked and West had to win with A♣. Another club was led, South winning with K♣. Now, when declarer played 9♥ to A♥, both J♥ and 10♥ fell, and all dummy's hearts were winners. 4S made.

Let's try to sort this out. When declarer starts playing out his trumps, West has an easy time: he can follow to three rounds, and then throw three diamonds away, playing 6♦, 9♦, J♦ – the lowest one each time – indicating interest in the lower-ranking suit – clubs – rather than hearts (see page 156). This is crucial information for East who can now relax about his clubs. East wants to retain a diamond as leading away from Q♣ with J♣ to his right, runs the risk (realised on this deal) of promoting J♣ into a stronger card.

So, now, East follows to the first round of trumps, throws two diamonds away on trumps 2 and 3, and then pitches his clubs. He can drop 10♦, 7♦ to indicate interest in hearts, but it is unlikely to be important to West.

Now, when declarer tries the heart finesse and East wins his K♥, he can exit with his last diamond, which South must trump. What can declarer do now? Nothing. He still has a heart to lose and at least one club. 4S defeated.

That is why is it so important to pay attention to partner's discards. Once West has indicated interest in clubs, East can happily part with three diamonds and two clubs. This may help South to make an extra club trick, but it won't give up the contract.

This next hand should be a simple one for the defence but, when it was played, I noticed that many South players made 3H. Like an earlier hand, East comes under pressure when South starts to play off trumps.

Let me show you what happened:

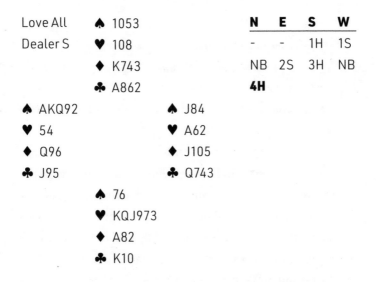

		N	E	S	W
Love All		-	-	1H	1S
Dealer S		NB	2S	3H	NB
		4H			

North probably shouldn't bid 4H, but having remained silent with 8pts and now knowing that his partner held at least six hearts, perhaps he thought that he might have just the correct cards.

West leads A♠, K♠ and Q♠. Declarer must lose A♥, and a diamond. But, when South ruffed, and played a trump, East won and returned another a trump. Declarer drew the final trump and played one more round. East, concerned that ♦J105 might be crucial, discarded two low clubs, and now South played K♣, 5♣ to dummy's A♣ and ruffed a low club in hand with his final trump. This felled West's clubs and South went back to dummy with K♦ and cashed his now winning 8♣, on which he threw his diamond loser.

The key here is that, whilst it is possible that ♦J10x is important, East has a defensive key role to play:

Defenders must strive to keep similar length
to declarer's and dummy's long suits.

To do this, you must look at dummy, remember the auction, and watch your partner's discards.

Using Suit-Preference discards here, West can discard first 9♠, then 2♠ – indicating more interest in the higher ranking of the two remaining suits (diamonds, opposed to clubs). Immediately, this should reassure East that he can pitch diamonds and protect the 4-card club suit to guard against dummy's 4-card club suit becoming established. On the fifth round of trumps, West should pitch 5♣.

So, in simple terms, whichever suit your partner indicates he has interest in – or does not discard – is the one you can throw away and, the suit your partner is discarding is the one you should hang on to.

If you look at the forthcoming pages about showing count in a suit, this can help you to think about the shape of the declarer's hand, and this information alone may guide you as to which suits to retain and which can be safely discarded.

♠ ♥
♦ ♣

Some people have all the luck…

One elegant lady at the club where I played most of my rubber bridge was a rare bird indeed: she knew she was lucky; she constantly commented on it, often apologising for picking up huge hands, game after game. She and her husband were very wealthy, enjoyed great health, and an enviable lifestyle.

This lady and her bridge partner joined me on a cruise of the Far East where I was in charge of the small, but comfortable card room aboard. They won all the prizes, and she won the ship's sweepstake. On the flight home, she was upgraded to first class.

Others are less fortunate – or think they are. In the same club, in the same card room, there was a lady who never stopped complaining about her perfectly average cards. When she lost, she moaned. When she won, she was upset that it wasn't by more. When she made a grand slam, it was a problem that she was never vulnerable when she picked up good cards.

This attitude reached its apogee on one occasion when I played against her. My partner and I had bid 4H and, after a mis-defence by our opponents, I made the game and rubber. The unlucky character threw her remaining cards on the table in disgust and uttered the immortal line:

"I had a complete Yarborough apart from three aces."

(I promise you, it is true)

Communicating with partner

Defence can be an exciting and challenging part of the game, providing you have something in your hand. At rubber bridge, Chicago or Teams, your only aim is to try to beat your opponent's contract – even if you give up an overtrick in striving to do so. At duplicate bridge, if your side can take one defensive trick more than others sitting the same direction as you, you will get a good result.

To help your partnership to succeed, some communication is required between you. This we achieve by using signals: playing a particular card in the suit that partner leads or you lead, and with discards: when you cannot follow suit and you throw away a card.

Let's look at a simple but, in my opinion, a powerful method of playing signals and discards.

Signals

When partner leads an ace, or partner leads and the first opponent to play, plays an ace, you throw a high card to say that you like the lead; a low card to say that you dislike the lead. Ace Asks for Attitude.

When partner leads anything else, and we are not involved in trying to win the trick, we show how many cards we hold in the suit. This is known as Showing Count.

Showing count

We play that to drop a high card in the suit shows an even number of cards, usually 2 or 4.

When we drop our lowest card, this indicates an odd number of cards, usually 3 (rarely, 5).

Let's look at both the basic attitude signal and basic count signal in context:

Dealer S	♠ J53		N	E	S	W
Love All	♥ A1082		-	-	1H	NB
	♦ 543		2H	NB	3H	NB
	♣ A86		**4H**			

♠ 10872		♠ A94
♥ 43		♥ 65
♦ AK62		♦ J107
♣ 1074		♣ QJ932

	♠ KQ6	
	♥ KQJ97	
	♦ Q98	
	♣ K5	

West leads A♦, promising K♦, and asking for an attitude signal. If East holds a doubleton or Q♦, she plays the highest diamond she can afford. This encourages partner to lead K♦ and a third diamond. With any other holding, she plays the lowest card in the suit, to discourage partner from laying down K♦.

On this deal, at trick 1, East drops 7♦ which, at first glance, seems a high card. However:

> *The size of the card partner plays should always*
> *be analysed within the context of the other*
> *cards visible or previously played cards.*

Here, a cursory study of the other visible diamonds reveals that dummy holds ♦543, West herself, ♦62. Therefore, East's 7♦ is definitely her lowest and so she is discouraging West from laying down K♦ and leading a third one (West can ignore this signal if she holds ♦AKQ – now, it is safe to cash K♦ also).

On this deal, if East-West do not signal and correctly interpret the signal, they will give away the contract. If, having led A♦, West continues with K♦, this sets up South's Q♦ as a trick, and South loses only two diamonds and A♠.

Alternatively, if West heeds East's discouraging signal and switches to any other suit at trick 2 (a trump seems eminently reasonable), South cannot avoid losing all three of her diamonds and A♠. At some later stage, East will return J♦ and declarer will either play low, allowing J♦ to win, and then lose K♦ – or she will cover J♦ with Q♦, losing to West's K♦ and East's 10♦ will take the third round.

N/S Game	♠ 82		**N**	**E**	**S**	**W**
Dealer S	♥ 864		-	-	2NT	NB
	♦ 653		**3NT**			
	♣ KQJ96					

♠ AJ4		♠ K973
♥ J10972		♥ 53
♦ 94		♦ 10872
♣ 852		♣ A74

	♠ Q1065	
	♥ AKQ	
	♦ AKQJ	
	♣ 103	

West leads J♥ against 3NT. Declarer has three hearts and four diamond tricks. He is unlikely to score a spade trick but, if he can make two club tricks, he will be home.

East and West should be paying very careful attention to the club suit. There is no other entry to the dummy hand, so East must ensure that he takes his A♣ only when he is certain the South holds no more clubs.

Declarer wins the lead and plays 10♣. West, showing count, drops 2♣ (showing an odd number, almost always three cards), and dummy plays low. If East won his A♣ now, when South regained the lead, he would score four club tricks. So, East ducks. Declarer leads 3♣ from hand and West now plays 5♣ (some prefer to play 10♣ next). When dummy's 9♣ in played, East must win his A♣ now. If he ducks a second time, he has given declarer two club tricks and his contract.

However, from the count signal he has given, East knows that West started with three clubs. Some basic arithmetic confirms the position: 5 clubs in dummy, 3 in East's hand; 3 in West's hand = South started with only two clubs.

So, East wins the second round of clubs with A♣ and returns a heart. No matter how hard declarer tries, he cannot get to dummy to enjoy his club winners and, unless East-West are *non compos mentis*, he will not score a spade trick and, so, 3NT fails.

Without West's count signal, East could only guess what to do.

Discards

We play that we throw away what we don't want.

The first time we cannot follow suit, we throw away a card from the suit which is of least interest to us.

In addition, we attach a **Suit-Preference** meaning to the discard, where the size of the card you throw away indicates which of the other suits you want led instead; a high card asking for the higher-ranking suit; a low card asking for the lower-ranking suit.

♠ AQ5   Imagine that your opponents are in 4H. On the
♥ 4   second round of trumps, you have the chance to
               make a discard. You will throw 9♣. This says that
♦ J5432 you do not want your partner to lead a club, but
♣ 9632   since this is a high card, you want her to play the
               higher-ranking of the remaining suits: spades,
               opposed to diamonds.

I strongly suggest playing these discards against both suit and NT contracts.

You also use the Suit Preference system as a signal.

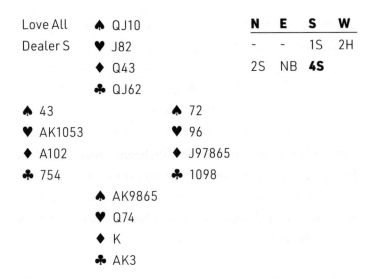

♠ QJ10
♥ J82
♦ Q43
♣ QJ62

Love All
Dealer S

N	E	S	W
-	-	1S	2H
2S	NB	**4S**	

♠ 43
♥ AK1053
♦ A102
♣ 754

♠ 72
♥ 96
♦ J97865
♣ 1098

♠ AK9865
♥ Q74
♦ K
♣ AK3

West leads A♥ and watches for East's attitude signal. East drops 9♥, which is a high card, indicating that he holds either Q♥ or a doubleton heart. Either way, he wants West to cash K♥ and lead a third round. West does lay down K♥ and, now, he must decide which suit he would like his partner to return if he ruffs the third round of the suit.

If you expect your partner to trump the lead of a suit, the size of the card you lead is a Suit-Preference signal as to which suit you would like returned.

With both the led suit and the trump suit out of the picture, the choice here lies between a club and a diamond. If West has wanted partner to lead a club, he would play his lowest remaining heart for East to trump. If, as here, West wants partner to return a diamond, he plays his highest remaining heart.

High card asks for higher ranking suit.

Low card asks for lower ranking suit.

This is incredibly simple, yet very effective. All you have to do is to give the signal and hope that partner is watching for it.

Here, at trick 3, West leads 10♥, East ruffs, interprets the signal and returns a diamond. Contract defeated.

If East isn't paying attention and returns a club, declarer wins, draws trumps, and throws K♦ away from his hand on dummy's fourth club. Contract made.

There is another occasion, in no-trump contracts, where you can use this Suit Preference Signal.

Love All	♠ QJ4		
Dealer S	♥ 1063		
	♦ 95		
	♣ AQ1072		

N	E	S	W
-	-	1D	NB
2C	NB	**3NT**	

♠ 32		♠ 10987	
♥ K9752		♥ A4	
♦ A64		♦ 10832	
♣ 863		♣ K54	

♠ AK65	
♥ QJ8	
♦ KQJ7	
♣ J9	

West leads 5♥ against South's 3NT contract. East wins with A♥ and returns 4♥, which West wins. West now knows that she must push out declarer's winner in order to establish two further heart tricks. With which card does she do this?

Of course, it doesn't matter to West whether she plays 9♥, 7♥ or 2♥. But, to East it will matter a great deal because:

When clearing a suit in no-trumps, the size of the card chosen indicates in which of the remaining suits the leader's entry lies.

Here, West's entry lies in diamonds, the lower-ranking suit, so he clears the suit by playing 2♥.

Clubs, so strong in dummy, are clearly out of the picture so, when East wins K♣, he should now know to lead a diamond and not a spade, even though South opened with that suit.

Declarer wins the third heart with Q♥, and leads J♣ and, when West plays 6♣ (the higher of his two cards to show count – and even number), South plays lows from dummy, and East wins with K♣. If East hasn't been paying attention and switches to a spade, South wins, cashes four spades, four clubs and Q♥ and makes his contract.

If East correctly leads a diamonds, West wins, cashes two further heart winners and defeats the contract by two tricks…

The duty of the leader's partner

When your partner leads a suit against a NT contract, it is usually a long suit. He wants you to win the trick (or regain the lead as soon as possible) and return the suit to him.

As the partner of the leader, your duty is to win a trick as soon as possible and lead back partner's suit (unless, by looking at the dummy, you discern that partner's lead turned out not to be the best).

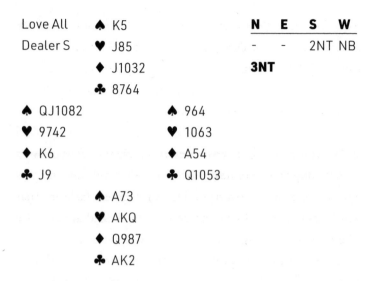

This is a deal I set my more experienced students and, sadly, it almost always passes them by.

West leads Q♠. Declarer has seven top tricks, and can establish two more from the diamond suit, but the race is on between the two sides to see who can establish their suit first.

Declarer ducks Q♠ in both hands and wins the continuation perforce with dummy's K♠. He now leads 2♦ from dummy. Most East players lazily follow low and West must win with his K♦. He plays a third round of spades, knocking out South's A♠ but, now, when declarer plays diamonds again, East wins and has no spades left to lead.

If we replay that hand, this time remember the mantra:

As the partner of the leader, your duty is to win a trick as soon as possible and lead back partner's suit.

Now, East should rise with A♦ the moment the suit is breached, and return his spade, clearing the suit. When West subsequently wins with K♦, he can cash his winning spades and defeat the contract.

Easy, and logical, really, isn't it?

What, you may ask, if East rises with A♦ and West's K♦ is a singleton? You were never defeating 3NT anyway and you have given away an overtrick in a very expert fashion, that will be appreciated by your teachers, peers, and anyone else who knows anything about this wonderful game.

I would like to reveal, privately to you that, as your all-knowing oracle, I make (rather too many) mistakes at the bridge table. In my defence, these are expert mistakes; my silly, careless, mistakes are only made after a great deal of thought! We are all trying our best – or should be – and this is a fantastically difficult game to play well, let alone perfectly. As long as your partner keeps an open, questioning mind and is trying to concentrate, forgive them anything and everything.

If your partner isn't paying any attention, find yourself a new partner.

Lead of ace of against NT contracts

A rare lead, usually made exclusively from AKx.

With no decent long suit of her own, partner leads the ace to see whether you like it – <u>Ace is for Attitude</u> – or dislike it.

Play a high card to encourage; a low card to discourage.

Let's see this in action:

Love All	♠ KQ6		**N**	**E**	**S**	**W**

Love All ♠ KQ6

Dealer S ♥ 87

    ♦ KQ1094

    ♣ A63

N	E	S	W
-	-	1NT	NB
3NT			

♠ 1082   ♠ J43

♥ AK9   ♥ 106532

♦ 873   ♦ A52

♣ J972   ♣ 84

  ♠ A975

  ♥ QJ4

  ♦ J6

  ♣ KQ105

Players in the West seat who led a "text-book" fourth highest club, did not do very well. Declarer won with 10♣, pushed out A♦ and, unless East-West cashed their ♥AK then, never made them. 3NT made with one overtrick, or three overtricks.

> *The worst lead against a no-trump contract is to lead*
> *fourth-highest from a suit headed by the jack.*

It almost never works out well and often, as here, gives away a trick.

Leading jack from J1098, or fourth-highest from a 5 or 6-card suit is just fine.

Instead, let's look what happens when West leads A♥. East works out that as she holds five hearts, dummy two and West ♥AKx, declarer started with ♥QJx. Holding the key controlling card, A♦ (preventing the dummy's long suit from making any immediate tricks), East encourages West to continue playing hearts, by dropping 10♥ (playing 6♥ may not be entirely clear to partner).

West lays down K♥ and a third round, which South wins but, now, South only has eight tricks before having to attack diamonds. The moment she does, East hops up with A♦ and cashes her heart winners.

Covering an honour with an honour – or not

The reasons behind covering an opponent's honour card with your own honour card are:

✿ to stop the opponent winning a trick cheaply
✿ to push out a second honour from your opponent
✿ to endeavour to promote a lower card in your, or your partner's, hand, on the third or even fourth round.

If you are doubtful about any of these situations, lay them out on a table and play them through – it is vital to know how this works. This is the simplest example:

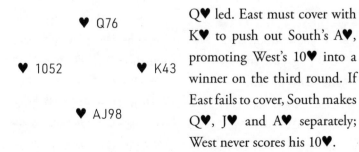

♥ Q76

♥ 1052   ♥ K43

♥ AJ98

Q♥ led. East must cover with K♥ to push out South's A♥, promoting West's 10♥ into a winner on the third round. If East fails to cover, South makes Q♥, J♥ and A♥ separately; West never scores his 10♥.

If you can't see an honour touching the one led, you should cover that honour immediately.

However, if the bidding tells you that you cannot promote anything in your partner's hand, do not cover.

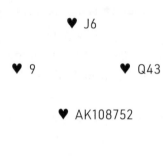

Imagine that South opens 1H; his partner responds 1NT and South then jumps to 4H. He must hold 6 or 7 hearts so if he plays J♥ from dummy, East must <u>not</u> cover – to do so cannot promote anything in his hand or partner's. If East plays low smoothly, South may well assume he does not hold the missing honour and play A♥ and K♥ hoping Q♥ will drop. Then, you score your Q♥!

Think about the bidding and be ready for when declarer or dummy lead an honour card, especially the trump suit.

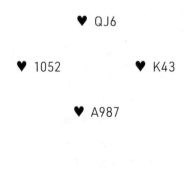

Q♥ led. East must not cover Q♥ but wait to cover J♥. If East covers Q♥ with K♥, South wins with A♥ and leads 9♥, catching West's 10♥ between his 9♥ and dummy's J♥. If East waits until J♥ is led to cover, West must make 10♥.

*Seeing more than one honour, do not cover
until the <u>last</u> of touching honours.*

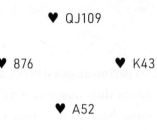

♥ QJ109

♥ 876   ♥ K43

♥ A52

Q♥ led. If you can see all touching cards, never cover at any point. Here, if you cover, you make it easy for South to make all 4 tricks; if you don't, he can only make three.

*If you can see all the touching cards,
do not cover <u>any</u> of them.*

♣ Q7

♣ 965   ♣ K432

♣ AJ108

Q♣ led. In a suit contract, as East cannot see a card touching dummy's Q♣, he should cover. In NTs, he should not cover as his K♣ will make eventually as South cannot finesse against him three times.

*In NT contracts, do not cover if you have sufficient
length to make a trick by right at a later stage.*

Since the purpose of covering your opponent's honour with your own is to promote a lower card into a winner for your side, you should not cover an honour with an honour if there is no possibility of that happening.

Be particularly careful about <u>not</u> covering an honour with an honour when your opponents are playing their trump suit.

Your opponents bid 1S – 4S and the declarer leads J♠. Should you cover?

♠ K743

♠ Q52

J♠ led

No. Partner cannot have more than two spades in her hand, so you cannot be promoting anything for her – or you. Play low smoothly and keep declarer guessing...

Generally, it is wrong to cover an honour with an honour when opponents are playing out an agreed trump suit.

This is one of these situations which you, as defenders, should be considering whilst declarer makes his plan. If declarer does not pause to make a plan then, at trick 1, you pause. Refuse to play to the first trick and have a good look at dummy, recall the auction and ask yourself what the declarer's likely plan will be.

If you hold a trump honour, work out how many trumps your partner will hold, and ask yourself whether it is right for you to cover a trump (or any other suit) honour if it is led.

Do not worry if you are not sure what to do – none of us are sure about anything at the bridge table – just take your time to think about it.

Do not take time to think if you only hold low cards, just get on with it.

Even if, by thinking, you give away the position of the high card, that is better than making a quick, un-thinking play. Most often, if you do the right thing, even if declarer knows that you hold a card, it will not help them unduly. Ideally, though, be ready for what the declarer might do.

Trump promotion

One technique definitely worth considering in defence is trump promotion. This involves leading a suit when you know that both your partner and declarer are now void. The intention being to get your partner to trump high, and declarer to over-trump. By using up a high trump from the declarer's hand, you promote a lower trump in your hand into a winner.

This is a classic example:

Dealer E	♠ 652
N/S Game	♥ Q109
	♦ AK10
	♣ Q764

N	E	S	W
-	NB	1S	2C
2NT	NB	**4S**	

♠ A10		♠ J7
♥ 7542		♥ J863
♦ 62		♦ 97543
♣ AK1083		♣ 92

	♠ KQ9843
	♥ AK
	♦ QJ8
	♣ J5

North's 2NT response isn't ideal, as his clubs aren't really good enough, but he holds 11pts and wants to bid something.

If you study the hand, you will see that South has only three losers: A♠ and ♣AK, so, 4S will make.

However, if West is imaginative, it can be defeated.

Watch: West leads A♣ and receives an encouraging 9♣ from East. West leads K♣ and, when both East and South follow, he knows that neither have any more clubs.

West's ♠A10 is only one trick but, if East holds any spade honour, West's holding can be promoted into two tricks. To this end, West leads 3♣ – a low one to ensure that East trumps in. Dummy plays 7♣ and East who, if he has remembered the bidding and counted up to thirteen, will know that South is also void, will realise that his partner is trying to make him trump. So, East ruffs with J♠. South must over-ruff with Q♠, and now West's ♠A10 will score two tricks. West beats South's K♠ with his ace, and South's 9♠ with his 10♠.

Contract defeated using a trump promotion.

Here, the defender sets up two trump tricks for himself:

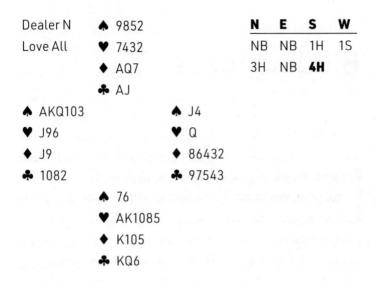

		N	E	S	W
Dealer N	♠ 9852	NB	NB	1H	1S
Love All	♥ 7432	3H	NB	**4H**	
	♦ AQ7				
	♣ AJ				

```
      ♠ 9852
      ♥ 7432
      ♦ AQ7
      ♣ AJ
♠ AKQ103        ♠ J4
♥ J96           ♥ Q
♦ J9            ♦ 86432
♣ 1082          ♣ 97543
      ♠ 76
      ♥ AK1085
      ♦ K105
      ♣ KQ6
```

West led A♠; East dropped J♠. West continued with K♠; East dropping 4♠.

What should West lead next?

A trump holding such as ♥Jxx can be promoted into a trick if partner can be made to ruff, even with 10♥, and a slightly better holding, such as here: ♥J96, can be transformed if partner has a high honour card.

Don't lead Q♠!

From the bidding, your partner ought to be able to count that South is also void but, even so, why give East a losing opportunity (if East does not trump declarer makes his contract).

Instead, at trick 3, West should lead 3♠, making East trump with Q♥. Now, what can South do? If she refuses to over-ruff, she has lost three tricks and will still lose J♥; if she does over-ruff, West's J♥ takes South's 10♥ and, later, West's 9♥ takes South's 8♥. One down due to an excellent trump promotion.

Bidding Ideas

played partnership rubber bridge at my local club, many years ago, with an elderly theatre friend of mine who thought he could act his way to being a good bridge player.

Unfortunately, the first pair we played against were the most argumentative players ever known, and were generally quite disruptive. I was appalled, and my partner was stiff and purple in the face with nerves. The first hand went quite well for us in an almost unbelievable way.

<pre>
                        ♠ K75
                        ♥ A6
                        ♦ A83
                        ♣ AQ1092
        ♠ A932   ♠ Q4
        ♥ 842   ♥ 10753
        ♦ J106   ♦ 97542
        ♣ 864   ♣ 73
                        ♠ J1086
                        ♥ KQJ9
                        ♦ KQ
                        ♣ KJ5
</pre>

Playing a 15–17pt Strong NT, South opened 1NT and, since even a minimum 15pts opposite North's 18pts (adding 1pt for the 5-card club suit), equals 33pts between the partnership, North bid 6NT.

My partner, shocked to be on lead against a slam on the very first hand, led fourth highest of his longest and strongest suit, 2♠.

> *Leading away from an ace against any*
> *slam is, generally, a really bad idea.*

On this occasion, it proved (an unintentional) masterstroke. Not believing anyone would make such a ill-advised lead, declarer played low from dummy. I played my Q♠, and was gobsmacked to find that I had won the first trick. I led back my 4♠ and partner took his A♠. One down.

This appalling, unforgivably bad lead, was the only one to beat the contract. The next hand featured one of the strangest auctions with which I have ever been involved.

Bear in mind that:

My partner is now shaking

The opponents are arguing over the last hand

That any underbid made is condoned if the next player passes or makes a bid

This is before bidding boxes, the room was hot, smoky and noisy

My partner is sitting West, and I am East

N	E	S	W
1D	1S	NB	1H
2D	NB	NB	2C
NB	2S	NB	2H
NB	NB	NB	

Yes, you read that correctly. My partner did indeed make *three* underbids, and not once was he corrected!

2H made, and it was the only contract that would have done. Brilliant bidding by my partner, and zero attention by the arguing pair, led to that all time classic.

Not a recommended bidding style, however…

Later on, at tea – taken in the bar, so my traumatised partner could down a few G and Ts – I told him about the hand.

"I don't remember a thing," he confessed. "And, if I'm really lucky, I'll remember even less tomorrow."

♠ ♥
♦ ♣

For me, there is no more wonderful feeling in bridge than when my partner and I judge an auction correctly because we are on the same wavelength.

At a very high level, this will be a mixture of many long hours of discussion and practice, combined with two brains working pretty much in sync.

At every other level of bridge, your duty is to come to some agreements over bidding methods and style, and then choose bids that are *clear to partner*.

As I have explained to good players over the years, there is no point making the correct bid if your partner does not understand it.

So, this section contains information about bidding understandings you may have, may want to have, or will agree not to play. But, it also contains bids which, when playing with new partners, should be understood globally, and are therefore a good idea with which to familiarise yourself.

Although my preferred system is Acol-based, with a Weak NT and 4-card major suits, many of these ideas apply equally to other systems. The most important element is that you find whatever you are playing to be logical (which many variations are, in my opinion, not). If your bids aren't logical, you won't be able to work out the best bid at the table, and that is no good at all…

Judging your hand

We were all taught to value our hand of thirteen cards by adding up our high-card points. Before we have heard what our partner, or the opponents, might be bidding, we can't really add on any points for shortages, but long suits are an asset. I like to add 1pt for every card over four in a long suit.

In simple terms, you require 12 high card points to open the bidding, unless you have a 6-card suit.

Then you might open with 10 or 11 high card points. Many students are taught the "Rule of 20" (if you don't know what it is, good – you have been spared useless information) to guide them whether or not to open the bidding, but this inaccurate rule merely replaces some simple thought.

♠ KJ
♥ J653
♦ Q8742
♣ A9

Would you open the bidding with this hand?

You have 11 high card points, but your two long suits are poor quality. If you open 1D and your partner responds, say, 1S, you cannot now show your hearts, as this would be a Reverse sequence (see page 237), so all you can re-bid is 2D, and that is not a great description of your hand.

♠ 4
♥ AJ986
♦ KQJ7
♣ 732

This hand is also 11pts but, here, you have all your values in your long suits and that creates tricks. You can open 1H and, unless partner supports your hearts, you can bid diamonds on the next round, indicating five and four in your two suits.

So, the first of these two hands is a clear-cut pass; the second, a reasonable opening bid.

High cards in long suits are more valuable
than high card in short suits.

Good bidding is shape-showing

There are many different bidding systems in the world but the reason why I love an Acol-based system is that it is natural, logical, and shape-showing. Some people try to complicate it but, really, if you keep it simple and pure, you have the best possible system. I play all the things I recommend in this book, at a reasonably high level, merely adding lots of infrequently occurring, but accuracy-improving, innovations.

The principle of our system is this:

If you have a balanced hand (no more than eight cards between your two longest suits) as opener, your plan is either to open 1NT or, if you are too strong to do that, to start with a 4 or 5-card suit, and then re-bid no-trumps. We will never freely bid two four card suits.

a)	♠ KJ4	b)	♠ KQ65	c)	♠ KQJ8	d)	♠ AJ87
	♥ Q93		♥ Q3		♥ J3		♥ KJ64
	♦ QJ1076		♦ AJ87		♦ J107		♦ AQ95
	♣ A10		♣ QJ9		♣ AQJ9		♣ 3

a) You have a balanced hand with 13pts (+1 for the 5-card diamond suit). Open 1NT.

b) You have a balanced hand, but you are too strong to open 1NT. So, open 1D and, unless your partner responds with spades, re-bid NTs at the lowest available level. If your partner responds 1H, do not bid 1S – that would show 5–4 in diamonds and spades and deny a balanced hand.

c) Open 1C and, even if your partner responds 1D, do not re-bid 1S. It is better to risk the heart position and re-bid NTs than to tie yourself in knots by lying about your shape.

d) Open 1H and, if partner responds 2C, rebid NTs, treating your hand as balanced. If partner responds anything else you can support him happily.

We have quite a few elements to look at here:

✿ With a 5-card minor suit, always open 1NT with 12–14pts and a balanced hand. I prefer never to open 1NT with a 5-card major suit but, if that's what you were taught, and you have no ambitions to get really good at bridge, then it is okay. If you aspire to play well, don't open 1NT with a 5-card major suit, however poor the quality. Indeed, the poorer the quality of the 5-card major suit, the more it is a good idea to have it as a trump suit (unless you have oodles of points).

✿ Never freely suggest two 4-card suits. Open one and plan to re-bid NTs, unless partner bids a major suit for which you have 4-card support. A 4–4 major suit fit is, really, what we seek so, if you have it, let your partner know.

✿ With two 4-card suits what should you open?

I play this simple method:

If one of my suits is hearts, I always start with 1H;

If one of my suits is spades, I never start with 1S (I bid the other suit).

If you plan only to bid one suit – and, with two 4-card suits, you do – then opening a low-ranking suit will keep the bidding lower. With four clubs and four hearts, you could choose to open 1C, but I like bidding hearts first.

✿   Don't open the bidding with a 4–4–4–1 hand unless you have a good 13pts (none of your points are in the singleton suit). This shape of hand often leads to angst and passing with 12 or a poor 13pts will save you much experience of that emotion.
Even with a 4–4–4–1 hand, do not bid two 4-card suits; just rebid no-trumps.

It is better to lie about your point-count, than about your shape. Shape is far more important.

Valuing no-trump hands

If you are going to reach thin, but good 3NT contracts, and not overbid on weaker hands, it is vital to value correctly your hand.

High Card Points are the same, but aces and kings are marginally less valuable than usual.

Queens and jacks are excellent values, as are tens, for which you should add half a point.

Long suits are wonderful in NT contracts and you should add 1pt for every card over four in a long suit.

AJ10 is a very strong holding at the top of a suit. Instead of it being worth 5pts, you can certainly add on a half point for the ten and, because it often provides two tricks, even opposite little cards in opener's hand, you can count it as 6pts.

AQ2, for example, will only make two tricks 50% of the time, and we count it as 6pts.

AJ10 makes two tricks 75% of the time, so it is definitely worth the same, if not more, than AQ2.

With what would you open on each of these hands?

a)	b)	c)	d)
♠ Q95	♠ KQ6	♠ Q96	♠ A10
♥ Q103	♥ Q1074	♥ A8	♥ K10
♦ QJ987	♦ AJ87	♦ Q107	♦ QJ87
♣ A10	♣ Q96	♣ KQJ105	♣ Q9864

a) You have 11pts, but don't forget to add two half points for your tens and an extra point for your 5-card diamond suit. It's a balanced hand worth 13pts in NTs, so open 1NT.

b) You are too strong to open 1NT, with 14pts, plus 10♥ and ♦AJ10. You can add half a point for the former and another point for the latter. Open 1H and re-bid NTs.

c) Open 1C. Adding half a point for 10♦ and a point for your 5-card club suit makes you too strong to open 1NT.

d) 1NT. You are not balanced, but you hold strong cards in your short major suits and length in the minors. This is a good description of your hand and opening 1NT will make it much harder for your opponents to intervene compared to opening 1C.

Playing a Weak NT (12–14pts) is wonderful for many reasons: it fits with our shape-showing system perfectly; it occurs far more often than a Strong NT; it is a mini pre-empt, making it more difficult for opponents to compete.

For suit contracts, you want aces and kings and singletons; queens and jacks are less important.

For NT contracts, you want queens and jacks, tens and nines; ideally a long minor suit. Aces and kings are slightly over-valued.

Your partner opens 1NT. With what would you respond with these hands?

a)	b)	c)	d)
♠ A53	♠ 108	♠ A986	♠ A10
♥ AK	♥ J74	♥ 63	♥ K96
♦ 7532	♦ 105	♦ AK7	♦ QJ7
♣ 8643	♣ AKQJ86	♣ K652	♣ Q10954

a) Pass*. You have aces and kings which are not so valuable and they are in short suits.

b) 3NT. You have 11 high card points, two half-points for the two tens and two extra points for your 6-card club suit. You may lose the first five tricks in a suit, but it is unlikely. Your partner holds zero points in clubs, so has at least 12pts in spades, hearts and diamonds.

c) Your hand contains only aces and kings and a small doubleton. Use Stayman to see whether partner holds a 4-card spade suit. If he does, bid 4S; if not, settle for 3NT. Respond 2C.

d) 3NT. An extra half point for 10♠ and an extra point for the 5-card club suit. Don't count a half point for 10♣ as well, as you have added for the 5-card suit.

Always support no-trumps with a long minor suit, not worrying if you hold a small doubleton(s) or even a singleton in a side suit. 3NT is far, far more likely to make than 5C or 5D.

Use Stayman on hands containing aces and kings, if you hold a poor doubleton or a singleton. See more of using the world's most popular bridge gadget in the Stayman section later on.

Armed now with the correct method of valuing hands that you plan to declare in NTs, you will end up in some thin 3NT contracts. Even if you make only 50% of them – and I bet you'll make more than that – it will represent a long-term gain over languishing in 1NT and 2NT.

* I played with the great Andrew Robson many years ago in the Mind Sports Olympiad in London, and this was my hand. I passed and, when dummy went down, Andrew nodded encouragingly. He played the hand brilliantly – as so often – and made ten tricks. I apologised.

When we looked at the score-card, we saw that everyone was in 3NT (he had 14pts) but several people had gone off, so we didn't get a complete zero on the hand. No one else made ten tricks.

"I would have passed too," Andrew told me reassuringly (he's a great partner).

And I would pass again if I'm dealt that hand – but not if I was playing with Andrew. The fact that I was playing with the best declarer in the room should, almost certainly, have swayed me.

Amazingly – and mainly because my partner played most of the hands – we won the event.

Valuing your hand correctly

As we have seen, the value of your hand changes as the bidding progresses, but how do you best value it before any bidding?

For suit contracts

1pt for every card over four in your long suit or suits.

Only count values for shortages when you are agreeing a suit with 4-card trump support.

Void 5pts, singleton 3pts, doubleton 1pt.

If the shortages are in the hand with the longer trumps, they are less valuable.

Void 3pts, singleton 2pts, doubleton 1pt.

For NT contracts

Half a point for every ten in your hand.
1pt for every card over four in your long suit.
AJ10 in any suit is worth 6pts.

The Rules of 19 or 20 – or any other rules – are largely useless.

The Losing Trick Count is excellent once you have found a fit, but *no use at all* at the outset of the auction.

The best way to assess your hand at the beginning is via high card points, plus points for length.
With strong hands and a long suit, potential playing tricks can also be used.

a)	b)	c)	d)
♠ J7	♠ AKJ954	♠ 3	♠ 93
♥ K984	♥ 76	♥ AQJ87	♥ AKQJ76
♦ AJ642	♦ K83	♦ KJ1095	♦ 82
♣ Q4	♣ 52	♣ 64	♣ AQJ

a) 11pts. You could open 1D, but you will never get to show hearts, because that would create a Reverse sequence. With little titbits in clubs and spades, this is not a good hand. At Duplicate bridge, you might open an off-centre 1NT (11pts, plus one extra for the fifth diamond). My preference would be to pass, and enter the auction later if the opponents bid the black suits and display weakness.

b) 11pts but, this time, a 6-card suit and not tiddly unsupported queens and jacks. This is well worth a 1S opening bid.

c) 11pts but all your values are concentrated in your two long suits. Pass is okay, but I would open 1H and prepare to rebid diamonds.

d) 17pts but, more importantly, a very high quality 6-card suit and the potential to make 8 or 9 tricks on your own. This hand is therefore worth a Strong 2 Opener.

Which suit to open

There are various theories, but I like the traditional one the best, because it leads to useful, simple-to-deduce, logical reasonings regarding the shape of your partner's hand.

> *And, in bridge, there is nothing so useful as*
> *knowing the shape of your partner's hand.*

I have intoned this mantra for forty-five years, and goodness knows how many times in classes.

With 15pts or more (since with 12–14, you would open 1NT) and two 4-card suits:

If one of them is hearts, always open 1H
If one of them is spades, never open 1S
If they are both minor suits, open the weaker one.

a)	b)	c)	d)
♠ J72	♠ KQ64	♠ AKJ3	♠ AJ
♥ K987	♥ AJ62	♥ 52	♥ Q97
♦ AJ64	♦ J3	♦ J964	♦ 8632
♣ A3	♣ A97	♣ AQ7	♣ AKQ10

a) 1NT. No problem.

b) 1H. Partner can now respond 1S and you find your 4–4 fit, whereas if you open 1S, partner cannot bid 2H without five of them.

c) 1D. Partner probably responds 1H; now you can rebid 1NT. If you open 1S, partner has to bid at the 2-level and you have to rebid 2NT. That isn't a problem, it's just wasteful of bidding space.

d) 1D. Your plan is to re-bid NTs and hopefully to play in a no-trump contract. Put the opponents off from leading your weak suit, and if partner bids 2D, she must have four of them, so you have your 8-card fit; if she bids 3D, you are re-bidding 3NT anyway.

With 11pts or more, with two 5-card suits:

Open the higher-ranking suit, unless you hold five clubs and five spades, when you must open 1C.

This is because, when you plan to bid two suits, it usually works out more economical to bid the higher-ranking suit first, followed by the lower-ranking suit.

This logic does not apply to clubs and spades because:

```
1C - 1H              1S - 2H
          whereas
1S                   3C
```

You can see that you can show 5–4 in clubs and spades at the 1-level and, when you bid for a third time, you bid spades again and this shows your 5–5 shape.

Whereas, if you bid spades first, to show your second suit now requires you to bid at the 3-level, which is a game forcing High-level Reverse, and therefore quite inappropriate if you just hold 11-15pts and 5–5 shape.

Or, to put it another way, one auction is space-saving, scientific, and logical – and the other is the opposite of all those things!

If you are 6–6 shape, just follow the above rule.

Tell me now – e-mail me, post on social media, shout it from the rooftops – if this is not clear. I think it's easy, but some of my students seems to disagree, since they are always asking me which suit to open.

After one particularly frustrating morning, I phoned two of my non-bridge playing friends. I said: "Do me a favour. I know that you won't know what I'm talking about, but please could you remember this and answer a question for me at the end of the week?"

I went on: "With two 4-card suits, always open hearts, never spades. With two 5-card suits, open the higher-ranking, except if you have clubs and spades."

With that, I put down the phone. At the end of the week, I called them both again.

"I've got four hearts and four diamonds," I told them. "Which should I open?"

A sigh proceeded. "You said with four hearts to open those, so hearts."

"And what about if I have four diamonds and four spades?"

"You said never spades, so I suppose the other one."

And, finally, I said, "What if I have five hearts and five clubs?"

Sounding really bored now: "You said the higher-ranking one unless it's spades and clubs, so whichever is the higher-ranking one."

"Thank you," I said joyously, and put down the phone. I am fully vindicated. Even people who have no idea about bridge can remember that.

And then, suddenly, my joy evaporated: I have been teaching some of my students for many years (some for many, many years) and I haven't yet found a way to teach them how to remember which suit to open. That's not their fault, it's mine.

But, my sweet fellow students of the green baize, I can't think of any other way to impart this key, basic knowledge, so please help me out here: just re-read this section until you really know it. That will serve a double purpose: it will improve both your bridge and my sleep patterns...

What should you open with a wildly distributional hand?

I don't often write about wild distributions, because they don't often come up, and there is a great deal of luck in how an auction develops on such hands. In the old days, players didn't compete so aggressively, so you had much more time to describe the shape of your hand. Modern bridge players know, however, that sitting in reverential silence will lead to bad scores in the long run, and they bid, and bid, and bid some more. And, then, when they're done bidding, they bid again.

Look at this hand from only a few weeks ago.

Dealer S	♠ -		**N**	**E**	**S**	**W**
N/S Game	♥ 97542		-	-	2C	3C
	♦ J8543		NB	5C	**5S**	
	♣ A32					

♠ 52	♠ 109863
♥ 63	♥ A
♦ A96	♦ KQ107
♣ KQ10976	♣ J84

♠ AKQJ74
♥ KQJ108
♦ 2
♣ 5

With a very likely 10 playing tricks, South opened a game-forcing 2C. At favourable vulnerability, West overcalled 3C, promising a 6-card suit, North passed (she might have doubled to show a solid stopper in clubs) and East jumped to 5C. Unable to describe her hand now, South simply had to compete with 5S, and got most unlucky with the dummy. A♥, A♦ and a spade trick meant that N/S went one down.

This is the problem with opening an artificial bid with relatively few points and great shape: your opponents can barrage you out of the auction.

Instead, South should open 1S.

Yes, it is possible that everyone will pass and North will hold a balanced 5pt hand and 4H or 4S will make, but holding a 6–5 hand makes is more likely there will be shape elsewhere and, these days, players don't like leaving their opponents to play at low levels.

The huge advantage of opening 1S is that you have bid one of your suits already. Now, if the auction runs 1S – 3C – NB – 5C, you can bid your other suit: 5H.

Here, your partner passes and you make 5H but, had she held similar length in spades and hearts, she could put you back to 5S.

So, with 6–5, 6–6 and 7–6 hands, unless you hold 20pts or so, try opening at the 1-level and then jumping in your second suit, or competing at whatever level you are pushed to. This way, you'll have bid both your suits and your partner can make her choice.

However, if you hold: ♠ AKQ86
                         ♥ AKQ95
                         ♦ A
                         ♣ 73

Make sure that you do open 2C, because if you start with 1S here, the chances of the auction running 1S - NB – NB - NB are far too high, and you really can't be squandering little beauties like this.

With weak hands, you will often do better to pass at your first turn, and re-enter the auction later with a take-out double, Unusual NT Overcall, or similar.

a)	b)	c)	d)
♠ AQ986	♠ QJ1064	♠ KJ84	♠ 6
♥ KJ987	♥ KJ10753	♥ 52	♥ -
♦ 64	♦ 2	♦ AJ9643	♦ KQ9732
♣ 3	♣ 7	♣ 7	♣ A86543

a) With all your values in your two suits, opening 1S here is fine. There may be problems if the hand is a misfit and an original pass might work well.

b) You might open a Weak 2H, or even 1H, but you will have difficulty describing your hand later. If you re-bid spades, it will be a reverse, promising 16pts or more. It is much superior to pass originally and enter the auction later, even if it is at the 3 or 4-level.

c) Pass. You don't have anywhere near an opening hand.

d) Again, pass may well prove best. After all, even if your opponents bid to 4H or 4S, you can still enter the auction but here, with all your values in your two suits and 6–6 distribution, I would open 1D and be prepared to rebid clubs, even if it is at the 5-level. With this hand, you should never be passing 3NT by your partner, nor 4H or 4S by your opponents: just keep bidding clubs and show your shape.

With a 2-suited hand, open the longer suit first (or the higher-ranking, unless you have spades and clubs) and then rebid the second suit again. The longer your second suit is, the longer your first suit must be in order for you to have opened with it first.

1D	1S	This shows 5–5 or longer in your two suits.
2C	2NT	
3C		

1S	2C	This shows 6–6 in spades and hearts. You have bid
2H	3C	hearts three times, promising six of them and, as
3H	3NT	you chose to open 1S initially, you must have as
4H		many spades as hearts.

1H	2D	This sequence shows five spades and therefore six
2S	2NT	hearts, since you opened the bidding with hearts.
3S		

Notice that, in every example, you bid the higher-ranking, or longer, suit first and then never bid it again. This is because as the second suit is shown to be longer, so the first suit must, logically promise more length also.

1S	2C	Finally, this sequence shows six spades and only
2H	2NT	four hearts. That is why you do not bid the hearts
3S		again. If you only held 5–4 in your two suits, you
		would pass or raise your partner's NT bid, or show
		3-card support for her clubs.

No-trump bidding with a long minor suit

When you hold a long minor suit, always think about playing in 3NT opposed to 5C or 5D. This next example is a question I've asked many thousands of times. Decide on your answer:

Partner opens 1NT (12–14). With what would you respond with this hand?

♠ 86

♥ J7

♦ AKQ542

♣ J93

Let's take a moment to consider the possible final contracts. 5D usually requires the equivalent of 27/28pts between the two hands. You're probably a bit short.

3NT only requires about 25/26pts between the partnership and that means here, even if partner only holds 12pts, you may well be able to make 9 tricks. You have 11 high card points, plus two more for your fifth and sixth diamonds. The only possible response to your partner is 3NT.

You are far too strong to make a weak take-out, and not nearly strong enough to make a slam try jump response of 3D. You know the limit of this hand, and that is a thin game in 3NT.

What if you don't make 3NT? So what? You will at least half the time, probably a good deal more often. That means that you bidding 3NT may not be right every time, but if you keep on raising NT bids with a long minor suit, you will get very rich in the long run.

Stopper-showing bids for no-trumps

For the same reasons outlined above, when you hold a fit in a minor suit, always seek to play in 3NT opposed to 5C or 5D.

To this end, you want to play Stopper-Showing Bids for NTs.

These bids used to be called "Minor-Suit Trial Bids", but since they are bids, showing stoppers, looking to play in a NT contract, my more modern name fits the bill rather better.

The principle is this: when a minor suit has been agreed, or emphasised, any new bid at the 2 or 3-level, shows a stopper(s) in that suit, and asks partner to bid the suit where she holds stoppers.

There are two key bridge rules to help you to remember these bids:

✿   With a minor-suit fit, always check for 3NT before committing yourself to playing in 5C/5D.

✿   Once you have agreed a suit, you can never have a different trump suit; although you might play in NTs.

♠ 652   The bidding runs 1C – 3C. You might make 5C,
♥ A7   but 3NT only requires 9 tricks, and may score
♦ A4   more at Duplicate. To succeed in no-trumps,
♣ AKJ753   you need partner to have at least one stopper

in spades. You now show where you hold a stopper and partner does the same. Bid them in the cheapest order. So, here, you bid 3D.

This shows a diamond stopper and asks partner to indicate where she holds stoppers: if partner has a stopper in both hearts and spades, she bids 3NT immediately; if he has a stopper in hearts, she bids 3H; a stopper in spades, she bids 3S.

If all the suits are covered, bid 3NT. If there is a suit not covered, then bid 4C or 5C.

1C-3C 3H	If a suit is left out in the cheapest order of bidding, this indicates that the player does not hold a stopper in that suit. So, here, opener has no stopper in diamonds.

When your partner opens 1C and you respond 3C and then partner makes a Stopper-showing Bid for NTs, you know that she is worried about diamonds. As you hold a stopper in both diamonds and spades, you can now bid 3NT.

♠ K92
♥ 732
♦ A84
♣ KJ75

Because your target is 3NT, you must hold sufficient points that your side may hold 25+pts between you.

Over the auction: 1D – 2D, opener would need the equivalent of 17pts+ to use a Stopper-Showing Bid.

Over the auction: 1C – 3C, opener would need the equivalent of 14pts+ to use a Stopper-Showing Bid.

a)   b)

♠ J75	♠ KQ3	♠ AQ	♠ K92
♥ AQ	♥ 96	♥ 42	♥ 853
♦ AQJ743	♦ K985	♦ KQ753	♦ AJ94
♣ A9	♣ 10632	♣ AQ87	♣ K52

1D	2D	1D	3D
2H*	2S	3S*	4C*
3NT		**5D**	

a) When diamonds are agreed weakly, opener's 2H bid shows 17pts+ and a heart stopper. Responder shows her stopper in spades, and now opener can bid 3NT safe in the knowledge that all four suits are covered.

b) When opener re-bids 3S, responder notes that hearts have been missed out: that must be the suit about which she is worried. Unable to help in hearts, responder knows that 3NT is not possible but, being strong, she bids 4C, showing values, and that encourages opener to bid the correct diamond contract.

There are two other occasions when Stopper Showing Bids for NTs can be adopted:

✿ Mid-auction minor suit agreement.

☼   After Opener's jump re-bid in a minor suit.

c)		d)	
♠ K5	♠ 983	♠ 6	♠ AJ972
♥ AQ765	♥ K2	♥ 942	♥ QJ3
♦ 53	♦ A74	♦ KQJ753	♦ A4
♣ A932	♣ KQJ85	♣ AKQ	♣ 852
1H	2C	1D	1S
3C	3D*	3D	3H*
3NT		**3NT**	

c)   Clubs are agreed, so now any new bid at the 2 or 3-level is a Stopper Showing Bid for NTs.

When 3D is bid, this shows a diamond stopper, and indicates nothing in spades. Opener has a spade stopper, so she re-bids 3NT.

d)   When opener jump re-bids to 3D, any new suit at the 3-level is a Stopper Showing Bid for NTs.

3H shows a heart stopper, but responder must be worried about the un-bid suit. Opener has that well-covered, so she can bid 3NT.

If I walked into a bridge club anywhere in the world (opposed to a social game at home, or sports club section) I would expect players to understand these bids as a matter of course. All good players know that to play in 5C or 5D is generally a mug's game, and striving to play in 3NT is the winning strategy. If they know that, and now so do you, then everyone's bridge will improve.

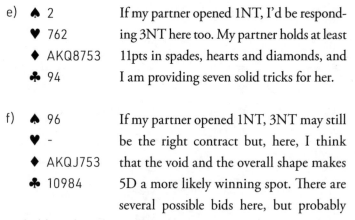

e) ♠ 2   If my partner opened 1NT, I'd be respond-
   ♥ 762   ing 3NT here too. My partner holds at least
   ♦ AKQ8753   11pts in spades, hearts and diamonds, and
   ♣ 94   I am providing seven solid tricks for her.

f) ♠ 96   If my partner opened 1NT, 3NT may still
   ♥ -   be the right contract but, here, I think
   ♦ AKQJ753   that the void and the overall shape makes
   ♣ 10984   5D a more likely winning spot. There are
                   several possible bids here, but probably
just bidding directly to 5D is the most practical.

Note to duplicate players: I'd still respond 3NT on this hand; if
you make it with an overtrick, you will get a great result. That
makes 3NT+1 the highest scoring contract, but not the safest one.
   I'll just say it one more time – to get it off my chest:

*If you have a long minor suit, or a fit in a minor suit,
always think first of playing in 3NT and only end
up in 5C or 5D if there isn't an alternative.*

Free bids and forced bids

It is very important to interpret every bid made – or not made
– in the context is which you find it.

Let me show you two very similar auctions, and ask you what
you would bid on each:

	a)					b)			
West	N	E	S	W		N	E	S	W
♠ AQJ63				1S					1S
♥ Q75	NB	2D	NB	?		NB	2D	2H	?
♦ 53									
♣ A92									

a) 2S. You opened the bidding, your partner has responded: you are forced to rebid, and 2S it must be.

b) Pass. You opened the bidding, your partner responded, and an opponent has overcalled. This changes everything.

If you were to pass, your partner automatically gets to bid again. Since you now no longer <u>have</u> to make a rebid, to do so would be a free bid, and therefore must show extra values or shape. Since you have neither you must pass here.

> *To open the bidding and then, when partner responds*
> *and an opponent intervenes, to pass promises a 5-card*
> *suit (rarely, six) with minimum opening points.*

To freely bid here would show six spades or a hand with extra values.

	a) **West**	b) **West**		N	E	S	W
	♠ KQJ864	♠ AQJ75					1S
	♥ A5	♥ KQ94		NB	2C	2D	?
	♦ 109	♦ 53					
	♣ Q87	♣ Q6					

a) 2S. Despite being minimum, you have a sixth spade and tolerance for partner's suit.

b) 2H. You have extra values, something in partner's suit, and you want to show your shape.

> *If you have a minimum hand, or you dislike your*
> *partner's bid suit, if you are allowed to pass, do so. To*
> *bid here is a free bid, promising extra values.*
> *If you have to bid, this is a forced bid and*
> *you do not show any extra values.*

With a weak hand, support partner's major-suit opening with three cards

Playing Acol, when partner opens 1S, she has a 5-card suit 97% of the time. This is because, if she had only four spades, with 12–14pts, she would open 1NT, and with 15–20pts with four spades and four cards in another suit, she would always open the other suit.

When partner opens 1H, she is much more likely only to hold four of them but still, with a weak hand, it is a good idea to support partner with 3-card support, since it raises the level of the bidding – making it harder for the opponents to compete, but also ensure that, if partner has five or more cards in her suit, she can continue competing.

So, whether partner opens 1H or 1S, to raise to 2H or 2S is correct on all these hands:

a)	b)	c)	d)
♠ J72	♠ 964	♠ 9743	♠ Q62
♥ K98	♥ 762	♥ 8652	♥ Q974
♦ QJ642	♦ 3	♦ A964	♦ 863
♣ 53	♣ AQ8653	♣ 3	♣ KQ5

a) The doubleton club makes raising the major suit superior to responding 1NT.

b) The singleton diamond makes even a 4–3 major-suit fit a good idea.

c) 4pts, plus a singleton, and 4-card support, is certainly strong enough for a simple raise.

d) Even with poor shape, you should support hearts with 4-card support and spades with 3-card support.

But, if partner opens 1H and this is your hand:

e)   ♠ Q96
  ♥ 874
  ♦ QJ105
  ♣ QJ3

e)   1NT is surely the better response. You have no shape, all your values are in queens and jacks, which strongly favour a NT contract and, if you can't ruff anything, little trumps can be problematic.

One of the huge advantages of playing this way is that you now have a really strong understanding of what these weak bids mean:

✪ A simple raise of a major suit promises 3-card support and 6–9pts (4/5pts with 4-card support) and nice shape.

✪ A simple raise of a minor suit always promises 4-card support and 6–9pts.

✪ A 1NT response always denies 3-card spade support and usually 3-card heart support.

Opener should not re-bid her major suit without six of them.

1NT response does not show a balanced hand

In many systems, a 1NT response is played on a far wider range of hands than in an Acol-based system.

However, our 1NT response is excellent, and simply denies sufficient points to change suit at the 2-level.

With what would you respond to partner's opening bid of 1H on each of these hands?

a)	b)	c)	d)
♠ 72	♠ J10	♠ 8543	♠ J106
♥ K98	♥ J2	♥ 42	♥ 4
♦ 8642	♦ 9743	♦ AJ96	♦ Q72
♣ A953	♣ AQ865	♣ J85	♣ KQ853

a) 2H. As discussed above.

b) 2C. You only have 8pts, but you have a doubleton honour in your partner's suit, a decent 5-card suit of your own – compare this with hand d).

c) 1S. You must show any 4-card major suit at the 1-level if you can.

d) 1NT. Again 8pts, but this time, you hate your partner's bid suit. This makes your hand poorer. You do not want your partner rebidding hearts without at least six of them.

And what about with these hands opposite a 1H opener?

e)	f)	g)	h)
♠ 63	♠ 973	♠ J543	♠ J63
♥ 75	♥ -	♥ 2	♥ -
♦ K8642	♦ 654	♦ Q1087	♦ QJ9872
♣ A974	♣ AQJ8652	♣ A964	♣ KQ53

e) 1NT. Not strong enough to bid at the 2-level.

f) 1NT. Not strong enough to respond at the 2-level, particularly because of the void in partner's suit. Respond 1NT and, if partner rebids 2H, or 2D, then bid 3C.

g) 1S. Don't forget always to bid a 4-card major suit at the 1-level.

h) 1NT. You have 9pts this time, but the void in your partner's suit makes your hand considerably worse. Just put on the brakes now. This way, if partner holds a 6-card heart suit with 15/16pts, she won't jump to 3H, but merely rebid 2H, which you will probably pass.

You are allowed to change the suit at the 2-level in response with 8pts, but it needs to be on a hand which is fitting with partner. If you have a doubleton honour or three cards in partner's opened suit, you can change the suit at the 2-level with as a few as 8HCP (high card points).

Otherwise, with a small doubleton or singleton in partner's suit, you need 9HCP; with a void in partner's suit, you need 10HCP.

If you have a weak hand with a long suit, you can respond 1NT and later bid your long suit. This shows a hand too weak initially to respond at the 2-level but containing and 6 or 7-card suit and a marked dislike for partner's suit(s).

This hand, from a recent duplicate event, proves the principle perfectly.

West	East	W	E
♠ AK8642	♠ 3	1S	1NT
♥ A75	♥ Q94	2S	3D
♦ 5	♦ KQJ1086	Pass	
♣ A94	♣ 752		

This is how my partner and I bid the hand. With spades breaking 4–2, and K♥ sitting over Q♥, nine tricks was the maximum.

When I looked at the other scores, I was amazed to see many pairs playing in 3S and even 4S, all going down; even 2S failed. When East responds 1NT, West knows that he has a poor hand with two spades or fewer. For this reason, West can largely write off game and quietly re-bid 2S opposed to anything more adventurous. East should reason that his entire hand could be useless in a spade contract (as it turned out to be) and should insist on diamonds being trumps.

When you respond 1NT and subsequently show your 6–7-card suit, partner should pass unless he has a fit with you and a maximum hand, containing perhaps 17pts or more.

And, just before we leave this section, I want to try to save your partnership some avoidable bad scores in a situation where, over the years, my opponents have given me so many easy good scores. What do you re-bid here?

West	W	E
♠ A94	1H	1NT
♥ AQ75	?	
♦ K63		
♣ QJ8		

The answer is Pass. You were planning to re-bid 1NT over a 1-level response, and partner has indeed responded at the 1-level and has denied having a hand stronger than a mis-fitting 9pts, more probably 6–8pts. Therefore, 1NT is high enough.

1H – 1NT   shows 17–18pts
2NT
1H – 1NT   shows 19–20pts
3NT

If you remember the above standard point-counts and apply them correctly after a 1NT response, you will save yourself – and more particularly, your partner – much angst.

With a weak hand, support partner's major suit opposed to re-bidding your minor suit

Experts look for 4–3 major fits far more than average players and ensure that if they play at the part-score level, they are in a 5–3 major suit fit, opposed to 1NT or 2C/2D.

The tip which leads to these superior situations is this:

If you open the bidding with 1C or 1D and your partner responds a 1H or 1S, with minimum you cannot rebid your suit (2C or 2D) if you hold 3-card support for your partner's major suit. You must support your partner's major suit.

You can rebid other suits, or jump to 3C/3D, but with hands such as these, to support partner's major suit will, in long run, prove most lucrative.

You open the bidding with 1C or 1D (whichever is appropriate); partner responds 1S:

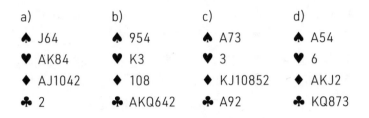

a)
♠ J64
♥ AK84
♦ AJ1042
♣ 2

b)
♠ 954
♥ K3
♦ 108
♣ AKQ642

c)
♠ A73
♥ 3
♦ KJ10852
♣ A92

d)
♠ A54
♥ 6
♦ AKJ2
♣ KQ873

a) Rebid 2S. Your 3-card support with a singleton means that, even if partner only hold four spades, a spade contract will play well.

b) Rebid 2S. Despite holding six clubs, supporting spades will work whenever partner holds a 5-card suit, or if she is strong, as she will continue to investigate for game.

c) Rebid 2S. Even with a 6-card suit, the 3-card spade support with a singleton makes the support of spades the best re-bid.

d) Rebid 2D. Here, you are too strong to re-bid 2S, and to bid diamonds now is a reverse sequence, forcing for one round and showing 5–4 in clubs and diamonds. When you later show 3-card spade support, you will have described your hand perfectly.

Some players are afraid of raising partner's major suit with only 3-card support (we would not even do this with a minor suit), but partner should always be aware that a simple raise from one to two of a major suit only promises 3-card support. Hence:

Partner opens 1D; you respond 1H, partner rebids 2H:

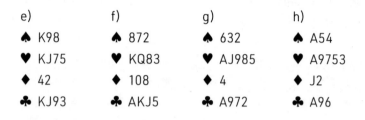

e)	f)	g)	h)
♠ K98	♠ 872	♠ 632	♠ A54
♥ KJ75	♥ KQ83	♥ AJ985	♥ A9753
♦ 42	♦ 108	♦ 4	♦ J2
♣ KJ93	♣ AKJ5	♣ A972	♣ A96

e) Bid 2NT. Holding only have four hearts, you cannot bid hearts again, so show your shape and point-count (good 10–12pts). If partner holds 4-card heart support, she can now bid 3H or 4H depending upon how weak she is. With only 3-card heart support, she can pass or raise to 3NT. If she holds six diamonds and a minimum hand, she also has the option of rebidding 3D.

f) Bid 3C. A new suit at the 3-level is 100% forcing. If partner has 4-card heart support, she can raise to 4H. With 3-card heart support, partner can rebid 3D to show a minimum hand with six diamonds, 3S (4SF) with one stopper in spades or, if she holds two spade stoppers, 3NT.

This does not promise 5–4 in hearts and clubs, because a suit has been agreed. You will always end up playing in hearts or no-trumps.

g) Pass. This is the perfect example of why re-bidding 2H with 3-card support is superior to re-bidding 2D with, even with a 6-card suit. The 5–3 heart fit will play beautifully and provide you with the best part-score available.

h) 4H. Whether partner has 3 or 4-card heart support, with your ace orientated hand, 4H will almost certainly play better than 3NT.

And, this gives me the chance to remind you that, as opener, the more you re-bid, the stronger you are.

You open 1C; partner responds 1S. What do you rebid now?

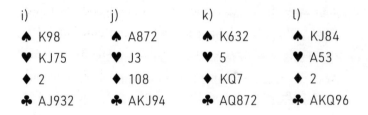

i)	j)	k)	l)
♠ K98	♠ A872	♠ K632	♠ KJ84
♥ KJ75	♥ J3	♥ 5	♥ A53
♦ 2	♦ 108	♦ KQ7	♦ 2
♣ AJ932	♣ AKJ94	♣ AQ872	♣ AKQ96

i) 2S. Minimum hand, may be 3-card support (12–14pts).

j) 2S. Minimum hand, with 4-card support.

k) 3S. Only 14pts, but an extra 3pts for the singleton heart (with four trumps), and maybe one extra for the fifth club too.

l) 4S (or 3D or 4D as a Splinter, if available). 17pts, plus 3 for the singleton diamond and one extra for the fifth club.

As opener, the better your hand when you support partner suit, the more you bid.

If you are not sure what to bid in a competitive auction and you have a strong hand, bid your opponents' suit

Bidding your opponents' suit is a wonderful way of waking your partner up. Playing social bridge, if you do this, your partner will often look especially clueless and quickly ask for a review of the auction.

If you bid your opponents' suit in response to your partner's overcall, it shows support and a strong, possibly game-going hand possibly game-going hand.

Opposite a take-out double, it shows two suits of the same rank, and asks partner to pick one to pick one.

At other times, bidding your opponents' suit shows game interest, or more, and a desire to elicit more information about your partner's hand.

Here is a typical bidding problem, easily solved by bidding the opposition's suit.

South	N	E	S	W
♠ Q65			1H	1S
♥ AQJ82	2C	NB	?	
♦ K3				
♣ A42				

You are very stuck for a bid here, since to rebid 2H would show a much weaker hand than you have. You would like to bid no-trumps, but you barely hold a stopper in spades. The solution is to bid 2S.

This says that you have a hand where game could be on (15pts+), you have no extra shape that you can describe, and that you probably have something in spades, but not sufficiently good cards to bid NTs yourself.

Your partner now describes her hand further – in very much the same way as after Fourth Suit Forcing.

✿ If she has a stopper in spades, she can now bid NTs; 2NT with 8–10pts; 3NT with 11pts or more.

✿ If she has no spade stopper but 3-card heart support, she can bid 3H.

✿ If she has five clubs and, say four diamonds, she can bid 3D.

✿ If she is minimum, with five or six clubs, she can re-bid 3C.

South	N	E	S	W
♠ K109	1D	2C	**?**	
♥ AQ2				
♦ K864				
♣ J103				

Here, you cannot bid 2D or 3D, since that would show weaker hands.

You could, possibly, jump to 5D, but you are not certain that this is the best contract: you might be going two down, or making 6D.

The solution is to bid 3C. This definitely shows an opening hand and is game forcing, since you have bid at the 3-level.

If partner holds something in clubs, such as Ax or Axx, or Kx or Kxx, or Qx or Qxx, she will rebid 3NT. If she holds nothing in clubs, she can describe her hand futher, rebidding 3D if minimum, showing a second suit, or even jumping if she is strong with a 6-card diamond suit, or if she is 6–5 in diamonds and a major suit.

So, if you bid your opponents' suit at 2-level, you will have sufficient points so that – at least – game will be on if partner is not minimum. If you bid your opponents suit at the 3-level, you will always have sufficient points for game.

Your partner first looks to see whether she has an honour(s) in the opponent's suit; if so, she rebids NTs.

If she does not, she describes her hand's distribution.

If you jump-bid your opponent's suit, or if you bid your opponents' suit at the 4-level (or very rarely at an even higher level) that it means something quite different. The way to remember this is that bidding your opponent's suit is often an attempt to reach 3NT, so bidding beyond that level must have a different meaning.

Jump-bidding your opponent's suit; bidding your opponent's suit at the 4-level

When you bid your opponents' suit at the lowest available level (at the 2 or 3-level), you are asking her to describe her hand further, often seeking a NT contract if she holds a stopper in the opposition suit.

However, when you jump in your opponents' suit, or bid it at the 4-level, you are indicating a hand where you have support for partner and you are too strong merely to bid game. This bid is nearly always a Splinter, showing a singleton (or, rarely, a void) in the bid suit and promising 4-card support for partner's suit.

Partner opens 1H; RHO overcalls 2C:

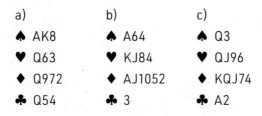

a)	b)	c)
♠ AK8	♠ A64	♠ Q3
♥ Q63	♥ KJ84	♥ QJ96
♦ Q972	♦ AJ1052	♦ KQJ74
♣ Q54	♣ 3	♣ A2

a) 3C. You could bid 2D, but a cue-bid of your opponent's suit clearly indicates that you want to be in game, and if partner holds ♣Ax or ♣Kx, 3NT may well play best.

b) 4C. Showing your singleton club and 4-card heart support.

c) 4C. Again, you could respond 2D but that should deny 4-card heart support. Ace and another is a rather superior singleton, and therefore the Splinter-esque bid here is best.

All about a 2C game-forcing opening

Long ago, you only opened 2C on a hand that contained 23pts or more.

These days, we should all know that a 2C opening shows either:

A balanced hand with 23pts or more

or

A distributional hand with game likely opposite almost nothing in partner's hand.

So, all these hands are game-forcing 2C opening bids

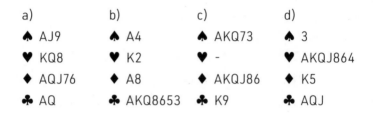

a)	b)	c)	d)
♠ AJ9	♠ A4	♠ AKQ73	♠ 3
♥ KQ8	♥ K2	♥ -	♥ AKQJ864
♦ AQJ76	♦ A8	♦ AKQJ86	♦ K5
♣ AQ	♣ AKQ8653	♣ K9	♣ AQJ

a) You open 2C and re-bid 2NT, showing 23–24pts.

b) You open 2C and rebid 3NT because, unless the club suit breaks really badly, you have nine tricks to take on any lead.

c) You open 2C and rebid diamonds. When you bid again, you show your spades: this promises 6–5 in diamonds and spades.

d) You open 2C and make a jump-rebid in hearts. This sets the trumps as hearts whether partner likes it or not, and asks partner to tell you about any ace he might hold in his hand.

Let's just clear up some rules about opening 2C and rebidding subsequently:

If you open 2C and rebid NTs, you show a balanced hand, or a balanced-ish hand with a long minor suit.

If you rebid 2NT, partner can use Stayman or Transfers if you usually play them opposite opening 1NT and 2NT bids.

If you open 2C and rebid a suit, partner will assume that it is a 6-card suit (very rarely, it may only be a solid 5-card suit). In any case, after a 2C opening bid, neither you nor your partner will ever bid a suit without at least five cards in it.

> *Following a 2C Opener, unless Stayman is*
> *subsequently used, nobody bids 4-card suits – ever.*

If you open 2C and, as your rebid, jump in a suit, that sets the suit as trumps – no argument. If the responder holds no ace in her hand, she just raises to game; if she does hold an ace, she bids that suit as a cue-bid.

So, you might have this auction:

West	**East**	W	E
♠ KQ	♠ 97654	2C	2D
♥ AKQJ986	♥ 2	3H	4C
♦ A	♦ J106	4NT	5D
♣ KQ8	♣ A1053	**6H**	

When West jump-rebids 3H, that says that hearts will trumps – no argument. Responder now bids any ace she holds (if she doesn't have one, she simply raises to 4H, and opener can pass).

Here, knowing that partner holds A♣ means that 6H must be making. West uses Blackwood to see if East has another ace but, when she doesn't, settles for the small slam.

Advanced response to 2C opening bid

I really like these simple so-called advanced responses to the 2C opening bid. They tell your partner what he needs to know and doesn't clog up the auction with unnecessary bidding. I highly recommend you adopt this system.

In response to a 2C opening bid:

2H = denies either an ace or king in your hand

2D = promises an ace or a king in your hand

2S, 3C, 3D = natural positive responses, promising 5-cards or more, headed by two of the top three honours: AKxxx, AQxxx, or KQxxx

2NT = positive response (as above) in hearts.

This means that when your partner responds 2H, you will know immediately whether or not to look for a slam.

Your 2NT rebid shows 23/24pts, and partner may pass if he holds 0 or 1pt.

Your 3NT rebid shows 25–28pts.

When partner responds 2D – promising an ace or king in his hand:

Your 2NT rebid shows 23pts+ and is 100% forcing to game. This allows more space to investigate using Stayman or Transfers.

Your 3NT rebid now shows 9 tricks, based on a long minor suit, with a stopper in every suit.

Although it is a little restrictive, keeping your positive responses to a 5-card suit or longer, headed by at least two of the top three honours, really tells partner where your values lie and helps him to judge how high to bid.

a)

	West	W	E		East
	♠ J4	2C	3D		♠ Q85
	♥ AKJ9863	3H	**4H**		♥ Q7
	♦ -	NB			♦ KQJ94
	♣ AKQ8				♣ 642

You can now pass, knowing that partner's values are in diamonds, with 2/3-card heart support and no A♠ or K♠. If partner had held good diamonds as well as something in spades and heart support, he would have bid more than just 4H.

With clubs splitting badly, ten tricks is the limit.

Whereas:

b)

	West	W	E		East
	♠ J4	2C	2S		♠ KQ1073
	♥ AKJ9863	3H	4H		♥ Q7
	♦ -	4NT	5C		♦ 8632
	♣ AKQ8	**6H**			♣ 54

Now, partner has shown five good spades, 2/3-card heart support and not much else. You can use RKCB and discover that partner does not hold a key-card. So his spades must be headed by ♠KQ. Bidding 6H is a bit of a gamble, but one that is probably worth the risk. Here, unless the opponents lead A♠, in which case you can claim the rest, you can cash ♣AK and ruff 8♣ with 7♥ before drawing all the trumps.

c)	**West**	W	E	**East**
	♠ AQJ754	2C	2H	♠ 106
	♥ AKQ86	2S	3C	♥ 732
	♦ 6	3H	3S	♦ QJ
	♣ 8	**4S**		♣ QJ9753

After the 2H instant double negative response, denying an ace or king in the hand, there cannot be a slam on, so West bids her shape, is shown simple preference and settles for game.

Whereas:

d)	**West**	W	E	**East**
	♠ AKJ109	2C	2D	♠ 6
	♥ AKQJ6	2S	2NT	♥ 9732
	♦ K5	3H	4H	♦ A864
	♣ 8	4NT	5D	♣ Q975
		6H		

An excellent contract, safely reached because West knows that East almost certainly holds two spades or fewer, with 3-card heart support or better, and at least K♣ or an ace in his hand.

Declarer should probably draw two round of trumps and then cash A♠ and ruff a low spade in dummy. He can then return to hand with K♦ to ruff another low spade in dummy.

If 10♥ has appeared, or Q♠ shows up early, it is very easy to judge.

Some people play that 2H shows 0–5pts and 2D 6pts, but I think this is a poor idea. In example c, East does have 6pts, but they are all worthless, whereas in example d, East only holds 5pts, but A♦ turns out to be huge.

2C openers generally want to know whether you have support for them, and whether you have an ace or king somewhere useful. If you don't, the 5-level or higher can be prudently avoided.

Pudding raises and splinters

A Pudding Raise is a simple bidding understanding that ensures that, whenever you hold 4-card support (or longer) for partner's major suit, you always show it immediately.

Hence, we have this table of responses whenever you have 4-card support for partner's major suit:

Supporting a major immediately with 4-card support

(failure to support immediately denies 4-card support)

1H – 2H	5–9pts (may be 3-card support)
1H – 3H	10–12pts (no singleton or void)
1H – 4H	0–9pts (weak raise with good distribution)
1H – 3NT	Pudding raise 13–16pts, no singleton or void.

Pudding raise

An immediate jump to 3NT can be played as a Pudding Raise. This shows a hand rich in high-card points (13–16pts), with four-card support or better, and lacking any singleton or void. It can be used opposite any opening bid. I think of it like my grandmother's puddings: rich and heavy in fruit, stodgy and shapeless in form. Opposite a 1H or 1S opening, your target will be 4H/4S or a slam; opposite a minor, your target may well be to play in 3NT.

If, as a responder, you think you want to play in 3NT, you won't jump there straight away. You should first change the suit, listen to partner's rebid and then make your decision as to whether to settle for 3NT or look for an alternative contract.

The direct jump to 3NT therefore has no other meaning and I recommend you to adopt this one.

If partner has a balanced hand, she can pass 3NT but, with any shape at all, she can bid on either to game in the agreed major suit, or look for a slam.

After intervention from your opponents, you should, as so often, cancel all conventional bids and revert to a natural system, meaning that the Pudding Raise is off.

With 12pts+, 4-card support for partner's major, simply bid your opponent's suit.

Partner opens the bidding with 1S; RHO passes. With what do you respond?

a)	b)	c)	d)
♠ QJ4	♠ K954	♠ AJ73	♠ QJ54
♥ KQ5	♥ QJ3	♥ AQ	♥ 963
♦ AJ10	♦ Q108	♦ J1085	♦ 2
♣ 8632	♣ KQ6	♣ Q94	♣ AKJ87

a) 2C. You don't yet know in which denomination, or at what level, you will play. If partner shows five spades and four hearts, or four diamonds, 4S or a slam might play best. If partner only has four spades and a flat hand, 3NT will be best and, by bidding clubs, you will have put off your opponents from leading your weak suit.

b) 3NT. A Pudding Raise, showing your shapeless hand with 4-card spade support. Partner can pass or, more often, convert to 4S, or look for a slam.

c) 3NT. Again, showing a shapeless hand with 4-card spade support. The doubleton heart may not prove to be a ruffing value and could work very well in NTs.

d) 4D. Apart from the 4-card spade support, this modest hand has two huge assets: the singleton diamond and the nice 5-card club suit. Game is certainly on and, if the singleton diamond sits opposite the ace, or even just little cards, a slam might be on. See below for the full explanation of a Splinter bid.

You open the bidding with 1H; LHO passes; partner responds 3NT. RHO passes.

What would you say now?

a)	b)	c)	d)
♠ AQ	♠ J5	♠ A	♠ A4
♥ AJ75	♥ QJ9873	♥ QJ875	♥ AKQ96
♦ K1042	♦ AKJ4	♦ KQJ93	♦ J86
♣ J94	♣ 6	♣ A6	♣ 73

a) Pass. You opened 1H, planning to rebid NTs and, despite partner holding 4-card heart support, 3NT could still be the best option. Bidding 4H is okay, but if partner holds low-ish clubs, and trumps break 4–1, it might not make when 3NT does.

b) 4H. You are weak, shapely, and the 4H game should be obvious.

c) 4NT. Hopefully, you are playing Roman Key-Card Blackwood, in which case, if partner holds 3 key-cards, plus K♣ or K♠, 7NT is cold. 6H seems pretty likely. Even if you play traditional Blackwood, this is the correct bid now.

4NT is definitely Blackwood since the 3NT Pudding Raise is not a natural bid of NTs and the Pudding Raise guarantees 4-card support for partner's major suit.

d) Pass or 4H. With so few points in hearts, partner has his values elsewhere. Bidding 4H is fine but, playing Duplicate pairs, I would pass and hope to make the same number of tricks in NTs as in hearts. You are very unlikely to be able to ruff a minor-suit loser in dummy, so 3NT looks to have the advantage:

you only need to make 9 tricks to score game and, the same number of tricks are quite likely in both hearts and no-trumps.

A Pudding Raise suggests, but does not promise, honours in every suit. Most importantly, it is showing 4-card support with 4–3–3–3 shape or 4–4–3–2 shape.

Splinters

Although this book is definitely not about lots of different, complex, bidding systems, I think that you should, at the very least, know what a Splinter bid is.

I recommend that you play them only to agree a major suit as an immediate response to an opening bid of 1H or 1S, or as an opener's rebid when responder has said 1H or 1S.

Splinters can also played to agree minor suits too but, since with a minor-suit fit, you want to end up in 3NT, I recommend that you do not play Splinters to agree a minor suit.

As a response to an opening 1H or 1S, a Splinter is a jump bid at the third available level.

It shows 10–15 high card points and a singleton (rarely, a void) in the suit bid. Of course, partner has to bid again. If he is not interested in a slam, he rebids his major suit.

Partner opens 1H; RHO passes. With what do you respond?

a)   b)   c)   d)
♠ 863   ♠ 5   ♠ AJ   ♠ -
♥ A975   ♥ Q8653   ♥ J987   ♥ KQ96
♦ AK1042   ♦ J10984   ♦ KQJ3   ♦ KQJ53
♣ 8   ♣ 6   ♣ J106   ♣ Q742

a) 4C. A classic Splinter bid, showing 4-card heart support, 10–15pts, and a singleton club.

b) 4H. Too weak for a Splinter. Opponents may well have 4S or 5C as possible contracts, so barrage them immediately.

c) 3NT. No singleton so, with 4-card support and 13pts, a Pudding Raise is perfect.

d) 3S. A Splinter usually occurs at the 4-level but here, with a spade void, you should bid at the third available level to indicate your hand. A Splinter will show a singleton 99% of the time and you should always assume that partner holds one card, and not a void.

Generally, you do not make a Splinter in a suit with a single-ton king, unless you hold at least 10pts in useful values in the other suits.

What do I do then, some of you may now be mouthing to the pages of this book, if I hold this hand?

1H –   ♠ KQJ9754
              ♥ 3
              ♦ Q82
              ♣ 63

You never pre-empt in a new suit once your partner has opened the bidding. The purpose of a pre-empt is to use up your opponent's bidding space, not your own. You should simply respond 1S and await partner's rebid. If he rebids 2H, you probably just bid 2S and that will likely end the auction. If he rebids 1NT, you can probably jump to 4S.

Platinum Rule in Bridge: *You only jump in an auction when you know in which denomination you will play – in other words, when you have support for partner's suit.*

Notice that both the Pudding Raise and the Splinter bids are big jumps in the auction. This is quite safe, as the responder knows that at least 4H or 4S is on, and neither the Pudding Raise, nor the Splinter bid takes you beyond that game level.

Reacting to a splinter bid

Before we look at the one other situation where we can use a Splinter, let's take a moment to assess how we should react to such a response:

You open 1H; RHO passes; partner responds by bidding 4C.

What do you think of your hand now?

a)	b)	c)	d)
♠ K98	♠ 5	♠ AQ7	♠ 4
♥ KJ75	♥ A98742	♥ QJ875	♥ AQ9653
♦ Q42	♦ AKQ	♦ 93	♦ AK
♣ AQ10	♣ A63	♣ KJ6	♣ 9873

a) The fact that your partner holds a singleton club is not of any interest to you playing with hearts as trumps. Your Q♣ and 10♣ will have to be ruffed in dummy, which means that they are wasted values. Just sign off in 4H.

b) Partner's singleton club looks great here for playing in hearts. You can play your A♣ to void dummy of clubs, trump both 6♣ and 3♣ with dummy's trumps and, providing that partner holds K♥ or A♠, 6H should be cold. If partner holds both A♠ and K♥, I'm bidding 7H – a contract we could never have reached without knowing that partner has a singleton club.

c) You have a minimum hand, K♣ and J♣ are wasted values since they will have to be ruffed. Just sign off in game, and play there.

d) Only 13pts, but what perfect shape. Partner's singleton club means that you will lose one club but can ruff the other three. If partner holds A♠ and K♥, 6H will be available. If partner holds the singleton A♣ also, 7H will be on. Again, these thin slams are unreachable without the use of Splinters.

To sum up then:

A splinter bid in a suit in which you hold only low cards or the ace is good news; a Splinter bid in a suit in which you hold king, queen or jack, usually means that those values are wasted, so that is bad news.

Using a splinter as an opener's rebid

The only thing to remember here is that, as a Splinter is forcing to game, and partner has only responded 1H or 1S and therefore may only hold a 4-card suit and 6pts or more, you have to be much stronger to use a Splinter as the opener than as the responder. You'll need the equivalent of 19/20pts. Since you can add 3pts on for a singleton in a side suit when you have 4-card support for partner's suit, this means that you will need 16pts high card points to make a Splinter as the opener.

You open 1D; LHO passes; partner responds 1S; RHO passes. What would you rebid now?

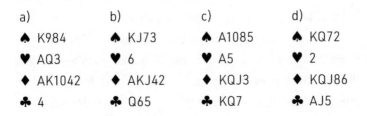

a)	b)	c)	d)
♠ K984	♠ KJ73	♠ A1085	♠ KQ72
♥ AQ3	♥ 6	♥ A5	♥ 2
♦ AK1042	♦ AKJ42	♦ KQJ3	♦ KQJ86
♣ 4	♣ Q65	♣ KQ7	♣ AJ5

a) 4C. A perfect hand for a Splinter: sufficient values for game even opposite only 6pts and a 4-card spade suit, singleton club.

b) 3S. Not sufficiently strong to go to game opposite a minimum response, but a nice shape so worth the jump to 3S.

c) 4S. As an opener's rebid, the more you bid, the stronger you are, so this shows 4-card spade support, no singleton or void, and 19/20pts.

d) 4H. Again, a lovely hand for a Splinter. Experienced players would bid only 3H here, but that would still be considered a Splinter. This is because, since a re-bid of 2H would be a reverse and 100% forcing, 3H cannot be a natural bid. Therefore, it takes on the meaning of a Splinter. If you and your partners understand this element, it is more economical only to bid 3H.

A 5–4–3–1 shaped hand always makes for a great dummy (providing the singleton isn't trumps) since it offers partner trump support, a singleton for ruffing, and a long suit to establish.

Any bid that is at a higher level than would have been natural and forcing, cannot be showing that suit. Here, if a simple rebid would have been a reverse, then a bid at a higher level is assumed to be a Splinter, agreeing partner's major suit.

Splinters are an excellent, relatively simple, addition to your standard system. Since to bid effectively, you must understand the importance of distribution, and an outside shortage in dummy with four trumps is one of the very best features to hold, to be able to show this is a significant advantage.

Roman key-card Blackwood

I teach my beginners this version of Blackwood, because it is so much better than traditional Blackwood, it would be a crime not to.

RKCB is superior to traditional Blackwood, as it identifies the trump king and queen and, when asking for kings, you can discover *which* king partner holds – which is essential for bidding grand slams.

Only use RKCB if you have the ace, king or a singleton in every suit, or believe that it is almost certain that your partner has a suit covered. Do not use RKCB if your hand contains a void. In these situations, use Cue-bids.

Having agreed a suit actually or by inference, 4NT asks how many of the five key-cards partner holds.

The five key-cards are the four aces, plus the trump king. The responses are as follows:

5C = 0 or 3 key-cards
5D = 1 or 4 key-cards
5H = 2 key-cards; <u>no</u> trump queen
5S = 2 key-cards, with the trump queen.

The reason why both 5H and 5S show 2 key-cards is because this is the most likely response. These bids then contain information about the trump queen. If partner responds 5C or 5D, you can still ask about the trump queen – see below.

I have never, ever, not known which number of key-cards partner holds when he responds 5C or 5D. The bidding prior to

RKCB will have indicated partner's strength. If you find that you do not know the difference between 0 or 3 and 1 or 4 key-cards, then you haven't done enough bidding before using RKCB.

If, between you, you hold all five key-cards *but only if you are interested in a grand slam*, you can ask about kings.

5NT asks partner to <u>name the suit</u> in which she holds a king. This will not include the trump king, since this is one of the five key-cards covered by the response to 4NT.

If partner has no king in an outside suit, she returns to the agreed suit at the lowest available level.

If partner has two kings, she can reply 6NT. This is a simple, but effective method. (Complicated versions are available.)

a)		b)	
♠ AKJ875	♠ Q62	♠ A8	♠ 975
♥ 102	♥ AK5	♥ AK973	♥ Q943
♦ A63	♦ 5	♦ KQ652	♦ A8
♣ K74	♣ AQ9863	♣ 4	♣ AJ76
1S	2C	1H	3H
3S	4NT	4NT	5S
5C	5NT	**6H**	
6C	**7S/7NT**		

a) When West jump-rebids 3S and East uses RKCB, spades are agreed by inference. West shows 0 or 3 key-cards. This must be three to justify his opening hand and jump-rebid.

East, knowing that 6S is a good contract but considering the grand slam, now bids 5NT, asking which kings West holds. 6C shows K♣. This solidifies East's clubs and now 7C, 7S, or the highest-scoring 7NT can be bid.

b) After an Acol raise to 3H, West uses RKCB. East indicates two key-cards, plus the trump queen. Since East cannot have enough points also to hold a king, West does not bother with 5NT, but bids 6H.

This additional feature is a more advanced element which not all players adopt. It will only be required very rarely, but can be crucial. 99% of all slam hands can be bid perfectly well without it.

Queen-Ask after 5C/5D response

If partner responds 5C or 5D to your 4NT RKCB enquiry, and you still wish to know whether she holds the trump queen, you can ask for this by bidding the next suit up from partner's reply, providing that it is not the agreed suit. If it is the agreed suit, bid the next suit up from that one.

✪ If partner does not have the trump queen, she returns to the agreed suit at the lowest available level.

✪ If partner does hold the trump queen, she then bids a suit in which she holds a king. In this way, she shows both the trump queen and a king which might be useful.

✪ If partner does not have an outside king, but she does have the trump queen, she jumps to 6-level in the agreed suit.

c)	♠ AKJ1098	♠ Q62	2C	2D
	♥ AK	♥ 73	2S	3S
	♦ KQ7	♦ A9652	4NT	5D
	♣ A3	♣ K84	5H	6C
			7NT	

c) When East raises to 3S, this shows a good hand. The 5D response indicates 1 or 4 key-cards. West bids the next suit up from the response to ask if East holds Q♠. East confirms this by now also showing, K♣, and West can now bid 7NT with total confidence. Had East held Q♠, but no outside king, she jumps to 6S.

Simple cue-bidding

Many people play bridge very happily without ever making a cue-bid. However, even played simply, they can be very useful, so here is a brief outline.

A cue-bid shows a first-round control (an ace or a void) in a suit, and indicates that you are looking for a slam. Partner is required to show any ace he may have in his hand.

You cannot show the ace of trumps using cue-bidding, because if you have no further aces to show, you must return to the agreed suit at the lowest available level.

You only instigate cue-bidding once a suit has been strongly agreed.

A cue-bid usually takes place at the 4-level, but there are some occasions where a cue-bid at the 3-level does occur.

The way to interpret a cue-bid is this: if you have agreed a suit strongly, then that suit (or, possibly no-trumps) must be the denomination in which you will play. Having agreed a suit strongly therefore, any new suit bid cannot be showing length in that suit, but instead will show an ace or void.

Why use a cue-bid, opposed to Roman Key-Card Blackwood?

a) ♠ A98743   1S - 3S
    ♥ KQ96   ?
    ♦ -
    ♣ AKJ

You have a great hand, but you cannot use Blackwood because you have a void in diamonds. If you bid 4NT here and partner shows you one ace – or one or two key-cards – you will not know whether this includes the crucial A♥, or the much less useful A♦.

Never initiate any kind of Blackwood
with a void in your hand.

Here, you should bid 4C.

You have agreed spades, so this new suit at the 4-level, must be a cue-bid.

In its simple form, cue-bidding always bids the most economical ace first.

So, if partner holds A♦ and A♥, she will be bid 4D.

If she only holds A♥, she will bid 4H – and you will know that she doesn't hold A♦.

Here, if partner holds A♦ she will bid 4D, and you will know that this card is largely wasted (you might use it to discard J♣ from hand), and you will then sign-off by bidding 4S.

Partner can now work out which suit you were worried about for a possible slam.

It can't be clubs – you showed A♣; it can't be diamonds – partner showed A♦, so you were obviously interested in A♥. If partner also holds A♥, she can now bid 5H (another cue-bid) or use some form of Blackwood herself.

a)		b)	
West	**East**	**West**	**East**
♠ A98743	♠ KJ62	♠ A98743	♠ QJ52
♥ KQ96	♥ A74	♥ KQ96	♥ 873
♦ -	♦ QJ5	♦ -	♦ AQ9
♣ AKJ	♣ 963	♣ AKJ	♣ Q6
1S	3S	1S	3S
4C*	4H*	4C*	4D*
4NT	5H	**4S**	
6S			

Here are two possible scenarios.

In a) East holds A♥ and denies A♦ (holding both, she would have bid 4D), so now the opener can use RKCB because she has discovered that partner does not hold A♦. When partner then shows two key-cards and no trump queen, opener can bid 6S with some confidence.

In b) responder shows A♦ so the opener, still worried about A♥, signs off in 4S. With no other ace to show, responder has no reason to bid again and passes.

A long-perpetuated myth is that you have to choose between cue-bidding and Blackwood. This is absolutely not the case. Often one checks that partner has control in a suit about which you are worried and, having found that she does, you then use RKCB.

c)		d)	
West	**East**	**West**	**East**
♠ A82	♠ 97	♠ A82	♠ KQ
♥ KQ976	♥ AJ83	♥ KQ976	♥ AJ83
♦ KQ3	♦ AJ654	♦ KQ3	♦ AJ654
♣ 54	♣ A2	♣ 54	♣ Q2
-	1D	-	1D
1H	3H	1H	3H
3S*	4C*	3S*	**4H**
4NT	5C		
5NT	**6H**		

c) Having agreed hearts strongly, West aims for a slam. He cannot use RKCB because he has no first or second round control in clubs, so he cue-bids 3S. Partner cue-bids 4C. Reassured that that the partnership does not have two quick club losers, West now uses RKCB to find out how many key-cards East holds. 5C shows either no key-cards or three and West knows that it is the latter.

5NT asks for kings, and returning to the agreed suit, denies any kings.

6H is rock solid whilst, at duplicate, 6NT would score best.

d) As before, West cue-bids 3S but, this time, East responds with a cue-bid of 4D – denying A♣.

West, fearing two quick club losers, signs off in 4H.

East knows that West must be worried about clubs. He isn't worried about spades because he cue-bid 3S; he won't be worried about diamonds, because East opened with that suit, and he's not too worried about hearts, because they have been bid and agreed.

So, clubs are West's worry and, if East holds ♣KQ or a singleton club, she can start up the auction again by using RKCB herself.

Cue-bidding shows first-round controls – aces and, very rarely, voids.

It asks partner to respond with her aces.

Failure to bid the cheapest suit denies an ace in that suit.

Think about which suit your partner might be worried about and then, if you hold a second-round control: a singleton, KQ, (or, providing the opening lead is coming around to you, even Kx) you can re-start the auction.

In more advanced variations of cue-bidding, you can bid your controls in a different order, you can show kings and singletons in a suit where the ace has already been cue-bid, and you can then apply more advanced understandings before deciding whether or not to bid a slam, and whether to bid at the 6 or 7-level. However, for the vast majority of the time, this simple version will serve you well.

Above all, do not be frightened by cue-bidding.

You have agreed a trump suit strongly and, if you have no ace to show, you simply tell partner this by returning to the agreed suit at the lowest available level.

Obviously, this is something to discuss carefully with your regular partner or group of friends before you start to play it.

Quantitative raises

Just a quickie here.

Any raise to 4NT when your partner's last bid was a natural bid of no-trumps is a Quantitative Raise. This says: partner, if you are minimum for your NT bid we do not have the required 33/34pts between us to make 6NT a good shot, so pass. If you are maximum for your range, we do have 33/34pts between us, so please bid 6NT.

West	W	E
♠ QJ6	–	2C
♥ K83	2D	2NT
♦ K742	6NT	
♣ J95		

Here, West could use a very advanced Super Quantitative Bid of 5NT (which says bid 6NT anyway and 7NT if maximum). But, since I have used this bid in battle twice in 40 years, I reckon it's too obscure to worry about. You know that you have 33pts minimum between you, so bid 6NT. If partner holds all four aces and 26pts or more, he would be entitled to bid 7NT if he's feeling in the mood.

West	W	E
♠ Q42	-	2C
♥ J108	2H	3NT
♦ 97	4NT	
♣ QJ874		

Here, East has shown 25–28pts and, if he is maximum for that range, you will have 33/34pts between you, so bidding 4NT asks partner to pass if minimum and bid 6NT is maximum.

In these following auctions, 4NT is a Quantitative Raise in every single one:

a)	b)	c)	d)
1NT – 4NT	2NT – 4NT	1H – 1S	1D – 2C
		1NT – 4NT	3NT – 4NT

a) opposite a 12–14pts 1NT opening, 4NT shows 19/20pts.

b) opposite a 20–22pts 2NT opening, 4NT shows 11/12pts.

c) opposite a 15–16pts 1NT rebid, 4NT shows about 18pts.

d) opposite a 17–19½pts 3NT rebid, 4NT shows about 14pts.

In each case, if opener is minimum, you will not hold 33/34pts between you, and he will pass, whereas if he is maximum for his range, you will hold 33/34pts, and partner will jump to 6NT.

The reverse

It's so simple once it clicks but, oh golly, how tough it is for teachers before they witness the light bulbs illuminating above their students' heads.

It doesn't help that "Reverse" is a complete misnomer.

This set of two bids by the opener (others can do it too, but the opener is the most significant) is about the use of space in an auction and how, if you are using up more space, you require more points to do it.

And, by space, I mean even one notch in the auction.

Let's use my (in)famous "Reversing Cod".

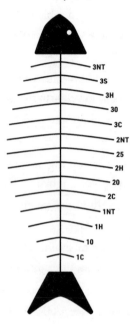

If, in order to show your second suit, you are lower down on the Reversing Cod than if you had re-bid your first suit, you are not promising any extra values over and above what you promised when you first opened the bidding.

If, in order to show your second suit, you must climb higher on the Reversing Cod than if you had re-bid your first suit, you <u>are</u> promising greater values: 16pts or more.

Look at this simple comparison:

a)	b)
1D - 1S	1D - 1S
2C	2H

Looking pessimistically, if partner is very weak (if he's stronger, you can relax) and needs to show simple preference back to your first bid suit notice that, in example a) partner can return you to diamonds at the 2-level whereas, in example b), he cannot bid merely 2D, since this would be an illegal underbid, and must bid 3D.

If the opener in example b) could only hold 12pts, you might find yourself at the 3-level in a mis-fit, being doubled, and failing for a big penalty.

To avoid this from happening, if your opener's rebid involves a bid higher on the Reversing Cod to show your second suit than if you were to rebid your first – even if that is by one notch – then you are making a reverse bid.

This reverse promises 16pts or more and is forcing for one round.

It always guarantees more cards in the first suit than in the second, usually 5 and 4.

What do you re-bid holding each of these opening hands?

a)	b)	c)	d)
♠ K983	♠ 73	♠ A1085	♠ 3
♥ 65	♥ KQJ8	♥ KJ7	♥ KQJ92
♦ AK1042	♦ AKJ42	♦ KQJ93	♦ AKJ874
♣ K7	♣ K6	♣ 2	♣ 5
1D- 1H	1D- 1S	1D - 2C	1D - 1S
?	?	?	?

a) 1S. This is not a reverse, because you are not bidding more than if you had rebid 2D. If weak, partner can still show simple preference at the 2-level.

b) 2H. This is a Reverse, because bidding 2H is one notch higher than re-bidding 2D, but you have 17pts and therefore you are strong enough to show your second suit.

c) 2NT. You are not strong enough to rebid 2S – a Reverse – since you only hold 14pts (and you have a singleton in partner's suit), but you are strong enough to rebid 2NT (15–16pts) because you can add on 1pt for the 5-card suit and half a point for your 10♠.

To rebid 2D would be too great an underbid.

d) 2H. A Reverse – and you only hold 14pts. But, what a hand! The more distributional you are, the less important points become. You have all your values in your long suits and, at your next turn, you will bid hearts a second time to show five, therefore promising six diamonds.

e) ♠ 84   You would love to rebid 2H, but this
    ♥ KQJ7   would be a reverse, greatly over-valuing
    ♦ AQ985   your hand. Therefore, you must just rebid
    ♣ 43   2D. It is the responder's duty to show
                      4-card major suits so, if you do hold a 4–4
    1D - 1S   heart fit, it should still be found.
    ?

Responding to a reverse

Once you have recognised that your partner has reversed, you can assume that she holds 16pts or more. She will assume that you have recognised the reverse and are bidding accordingly. Partner opens 1D; you respond 1S; partner rebids 2H. What will you bid next?

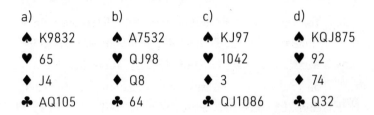

a)
♠ K9832
♥ 65
♦ J4
♣ AQ105

b)
♠ A7532
♥ QJ98
♦ Q8
♣ 64

c)
♠ KJ97
♥ 1042
♦ 3
♣ QJ1086

d)
♠ KQJ875
♥ 92
♦ 74
♣ Q32

a) 3NT. Partner has 16pts or more, you have 10pts and two stoppers in clubs. You must adjust your bid and go straight to game.

b) 4H. This time, you have an 8-card heart fit, all your points look to be useful (five are in partner's long suits and your outside value is an ace) and to bid any less than game would be pusillanimous.

c) 2NT. You correctly responded showing your major suit. Now, you must indicate good values in clubs, but without sufficient values to bid game. Partner should pass without the equivalent of 18pts or more.

d) 2S. A rebid of your own suit shows a marked dislike for partner's suits and a 6-card suit of your own. Partner may pass. Add in an outside ace or king and now you should bid 3S, which is forcing.

e) ♠ AJ983   Partner has reversed, promising 16pts,
    ♥ Q6   and you hold 10pts. You do not have
    ♦ J42   good enough clubs to bid 3NT yourself
    ♣ Q85   but, as you know that a game contract is
                   your destination, you can use Fourth Suit
    1D - 1S   Forcing to ask for further information
    2H - **3D**   from your partner.

Whereas to use Fourth Suit Forcing normally promises an opening hand, opposite a reverse (which promises 16pts or more) you only require a good 9pts or more to use 4SF.

And, finally:

You open 1D, partner responds 1S, you rebid 2H, and partner bids 3D. What, if anything, do you bid now?

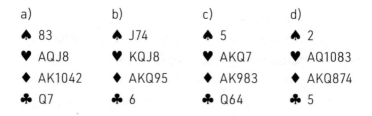

a)	b)	c)	d)
♠ 83	♠ J74	♠ 5	♠ 2
♥ AQJ8	♥ KQJ8	♥ AKQ7	♥ AQ1083
♦ AK1042	♦ AKQ95	♦ AK983	♦ AKQ874
♣ Q7	♣ 6	♣ Q64	♣ 5

Bear in mind that you have shown 5–4 and 16pts+ and forced partner to bid again. He has opted to show you simple preference. He may hold – but often won't – 3-card diamond support, usually it is merely a doubleton. He may have as few as 6pts.

a) Pass. You've shown your hand. If partner wanted to be in game, he should bid something more than simple preference back to your first suit.

b) 3S. Your shape warrants a further bid. If partner holds five spades, game could well be on, even opposite a minimum response. If partner holds four good spades, you might still make 4S. This further bid is a game try but, if minimum and unsuitable, partner may pass.

c) Pass. Yes, you have 18pts when you might only have held 16pts, but with a singleton in partner's suit, and a useless seeming Q♣, the hand does not seem to be coming together, so just pass.

d) 3H. This rebid of hearts confirms that you hold five of them and, therefore, as you chose to open 1D originally, you must have more diamonds: six of them.

With 6–5, you are usually worth an extra bid and here, now that your partner knows your shape, he can support you with 3-card heart support, or simply bid 4D (which you should pass) or 5D.

Other strong rebids

It is essential to distinguish between a minimum rebid and an encouraging one that shows extra length and strength.

a)	b)	c)	d)
♠ J7	♠ K2	♠ 84	♠ AQJ875
♥ Q85	♥ A8	♥ K9	♥ A6
♦ J4	♦ 753	♦ AJ7	♦ KJ5
♣ AQJ985	♣ AKJ864	♣ AKQJ64	♣ 92
1C - 1S	1C - 1S	1C - 1S	1S - 2D
?	?	?	?

a) 2C. You have a minimum opening hand so just make a simple rebid, showing 5+ clubs, with 11–14pts (if it is 14, it will be a bad 14pts, since with a hand containing a 5-card club suit and 14pts, you can add 1pts for your fifth club, in no-trumps your hand is worth 15pts and could therefore be described by a 1NT rebid).

This simple re-bid is usually 11–13pts only.

b) 3C. A jump-rebid shows a very good 14pts to 18pts and promises a 6-card suit.

c) 3NT. With a solid, or semi-solid, long minor suit, if you also hold a stopper in each of the unbid suits, rebid NTs immediately. Here, with 18pts, plus two extra points for your fifth and six clubs, you have the equivalent of 20pts, meaning you must rebid 3NT.

d) 3S. When partner responds at the 1-level, your jump-rebid is highly invitational and encouraging, but your partner can pass.

When partner responds at the 2-level and you make your jump rebid – as here – it is forcing for one round.

1H - 1S	1H - 2C
3H	**3H**
Invitational and encouraging.	Forcing for one round.

What about this sequence, frequently ignored or misunderstood.

1H - 2D
3C

When the opener shows his second suit at the 3-level, even without jumping, this is called a High-level Reverse. This is because, not only is it a reverse (forcing your partner to bid, quite likely at the 3-level), but the bidding is already at 3-level.

This sequence is forcing to game, so the opener will hold the equivalent of 18pts or more.

Any jump re-bid in a new suit by the opener is also forcing to game.

1S - 2C
3H

This sequence would usually show 5–5 in the major suits (or 6–5) with a hand where, now that responder has shown a minimum of 8pts (probably 9 or more) the opener is certain that he must end in game.

♠ ♥
♦ ♣

Back in the heyday of bridge, if your opponents held the better cards, it was deemed appropriate to sit back and let them bid unimpeded to their rightful contract. To try to throw them off their stride was simply not the *done thing*.

But bridge should not be a genteel, cucumber-sandwich-nibbling, fine-bone-china type of game. It is a mental contact sport, the equivalent of playing rugby sitting down.

Like so many other games, both physical and mental, aggression is required to unbalance your opponents.

I taught this to a weekly class of eight social-bridge ladies. They loved the freedom and fruitiness of the style and couldn't wait to try it out in the monthly battle between husbands and wives.

This randomly-dealt hand cropped up towards the end of the evening.

♠ QJ
♥ A64
♦ A753
♣ Q982

♠ 9875432
♥ 5
♦ 64
♣ J75

Partner opens 1NT (12–14). What is the likely final contract on this deal?

The answer, of course, is 4H.

No typos involved.

If you are looking only at the cards shown, you may not have spotted it but, if you are sitting South, and your partner opens 1NT (12–14) and your RHO passes, this is exactly what you should be thinking. So, what should you bid?

4S.

Immediately.

Your opponents must have 25pts between them. With partner's bid indicating where all your side's values are located, game is definitely on for them. You must try to stop them from bidding it. If you are playing transfers, don't use them. Just bid 4S right away. Now, you will leave your LHO – who surely holds a strong hand – with a really tough problem.

Let's look at the full layout:

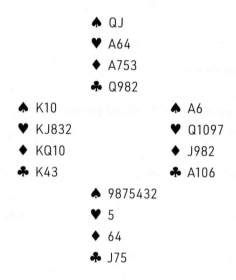

What will West bid over your 4S? He has 15pts, but you could easily have all the points his partner actually holds. To bid anything on the West cards here would be incredibly risky: pass will be right the vast majority of the time (especially as most people won't think as South does here).

East-West can make 4H with an overtrick (a club loser can be discarded from the West hand on East's fourth diamond). North-South go quietly three down on best defence (only two down if the defence isn't tight). If South bids directly to 4S, the contract is extremely unlikely to be doubled.

If West is really gung-ho, and does double, East probably bids 5H, which she makes, but North-South have lost nothing.

The time to think about these "advance sacrifices" is when you know that:

Your side hold at least a 9-card trump fit (so your opponents definitely hold a fit in at least one suit of their own too)

and

You know, for certain, that your opponents hold 25pts or more between them

and

your opponents haven't imparted much, if any, information about their hands.

If you are too strong, your opponents may not have game available to them, so going down – possibly doubled – will lead to a poor result for you.

If you do not hold at least a 9-card trump fit, your opponents may not have a big trump fit, so may not reach game anyway.

And, finally, the key to success here, is to make your barrage before your opponents have had a chance to communicate what they each hold. Don't bid 2S, then 3S, then 4S because, by that time, they'll be in the auction, working out that they hold the majority of the points, and then they *will* double you for penalties.

So, pre-emption of your opponents, when weak, and with a big fit in trumps.

You be surprised how often those conditions are met and you can get super-fruity.

Back to the ladies: they bid 4S, the husbands passed, the ladies went two down undoubled for a penalty of 100pts, and the men realised that they had been right royally swindled. They moaned, they groaned, they claimed it was unfair play, they said they weren't playing against the wives any more – this was surely cheating – and they whined. Oh god, the wives told me, they never stopped whining.

About four weeks later I received a phone call.

"Paul," said a very business-like, serious, chairman-of-the-board type voice. "We need to book you for a secret men's bridge lesson – immediately. Name your price!"

Overcalls and responses

When experts agree on anything, it's big news, but when bridge experts agree the world over to play in a certain way, that's amazing.

The good news is that for both overcalls and doubles, every-one who plays our kind of natural system, agrees that this is the best way to play these two vital competitive methods.

Because readers should be familiar with these techniques, I aim to revise what you know, fill any gaps and, perhaps, introduce you to one or two key elements with which you may not be familiar.

All Overcalls must be 5-cards or longer; no exceptions – ever.

At the 1-level, suit quality should be decent, and your point range is very wide: 7–17pts.

The vast majority of 1-level overcalls fall into the 8-12pt range.

At the 2-level, with a 5-card suit, you must have high quality; with a 6-card suit decent quality.

The point count is an opening hand: 12pts+ with a 5-card suit; 10pts+ with a 6-card suit.

Do not take risks overcalling at the 2-level; if the hand turns out to be a misfit, good opponents will trap you for a big penalty.

No one vulnerable. RHO opens 1H. What should you bid on each of these hands?

a)	b)	c)	d)
♠ KQJ108	♠ AKQ93	♠ A52	♠ A7
♥ 643	♥ 82	♥ Q74	♥ 532
♦ J105	♦ A85	♦ K3	♦ KQJ984
♣ 93	♣ KJ7	♣ Q9843	♣ J10

a) 1S. Minimum, but great suit quality.

b) 1S. Maximum, but other alternatives are not as good.

c) Pass. Terrible suit quality; not an opening hand.

d) 2D. Lovely 6-card suit; opening hand.

When your opponents have agreed a suit, a simple understanding clicks in: if they have an 8-card fit, so your side will also have an 8-card fit (97% of the time).

So, when your opponents have agreed a suit, you may bid with weaker hands than usual at the 2 and even the 3-levels.

The additional reason why this is safe to do, is that opponents who have agreed a suit are more likely to bid on in their own suit, than to think about defending or doubling you. If, routinely, you can push your opponents from their relaxing 2-level contract to the 3-level, you will defeat them more often. If you are left to play in your contract, if you make, that's great; if you go one down, that has stopped them from making their contract.

LHO opens 1H; your partner passes; RHO opponent raises to 2H:

e)	f)	g)	h)
♠ KJ852	♠ 93	♠ 542	♠ QJ92
♥ 983	♥ 2	♥ 1074	♥ 3
♦ AJ104	♦ 10985	♦ AKQJ8	♦ KQ96
♣ 3	♣ AKJ1043	♣ 63	♣ Q1087

e) 2S. Acceptable at the 2-level only because opponents have agreed a suit.

f) 3C. Your 6-card suit is lovely, it attracts the best lead from your partner, and opponents may well bid on.

g) 3D. Thin, but perfect quality suit: lead directing and unlikely to be doubled.

h) Double. You can make a take-out double on 2 or 3pts fewer than usual – when your opponents have agreed a suit.

If your opponents open at the 1-level and change suit at the 2-level, you will almost never overcall.

They have the majority of points between them, and have not found a fit. If they don't have a fit, neither will your side. Good players will be alert to looking for a chance to double any intervention. To overcall now, you will need a 6-card suit (never 5), and a really useful opening hand.

Responding to overcalls

There are some keys thoughts here:

✿ Support your partner's overcall or shut-up. Only very rarely do you want to change suit or respond no-trumps.

✿ Follow the Total Trumps Principle (TTP). Bid as many tricks as you have cards between you in the overcalled suit.

✿ If you have 3-card support or longer for partner's overcall, with an opening hand (we'll say 11pts+ here), you must distinguish this from the weaker hands where you are raising solely as a barrage: use an Unassuming Cue-bid.

LHO opens 1D; your partner overcalls 1S; RHO passes. What do you bid here?

a)	b)	c)	d)
♠ 8	♠ 754	♠ A52	♠ Q742
♥ Q643	♥ AJ82	♥ Q74	♥ 98653
♦ KJ5	♦ Q53	♦ 53	♦ 4
♣ AJ972	♣ J76	♣ J10986	♣ J107

a) Pass. Support or Shut-Up. The hand is, at the moment, a mis-fit: do not enter the auction.

b) Pass. Do not raise a 1-level overcall to the 2-level without an honour in partner's suit.

c) 2S. Weak, but perfect for a simple, barraging, raise. You have at least 8 trumps between you, so bid at the 8-trick level.

d) 3S. You have 9 trumps between you, so bid at the 9-trick level.

e)	f)	g)	h)
♠ K8432	♠ A54	♠ J32	♠ K5
♥ 64	♥ AK82	♥ KJ4	♥ A732
♦ 5	♦ 53	♦ QJ107	♦ A94
♣ J10972	♣ Q976	♣ QJ10	♣ A1063

e) 4S. You have 10 trumps between you, your opponents could easily have game on still and, if your partner is actually strong, your shape may make a thin game for your side.

f) 2D. An Unassuming Cue-bid (UCB). This bid of your opponent's suit at the lowest available level always says the same thing: I have ambitions in this auction, please tell me more about your hand. In response to an overcall, it says: I have 3-card support or better for you, with 11pts or more.

If you are minimum, there may not be game available but, if you are not minimum, game may be on. Describe your hand further. See the next section for how partner does this.

g) 1NT. You are showing 2 or 3-card support for partner's suit, two stoppers in the opponent's suit and about 10–12pts. You must be stronger than a usual response of 1NT, as partner could be as weak as 7pts (but will usually hold an average of about 10pts). Partner can pass, rebid spades with six of them, or raise you to a higher level.

h) 2D. You should have 3-card support or better to use an UCB, but you are far too good to give up on a game contract. Ask your partner to describe his hand further, and then make your decision.

How to rebid following an unassuming cue-bid

You have overcalled, and partner has bid the opponents' suit at the lowest available level. She is asking you to describe your hand further.

If you are minimum for your overcall, you do what you always do if your partner forces to bid again: rebid your suit at the lowest available level. Because you are being forced to bid, your rebid does not promise an extra card in the suit.

Minimum for a 1-level overcall would usually be about 7–9pts; non-minimum 10pts or more.

RHO opened 1D; you overcalled 1S, LHO passes, and partner bids 2D (UCB). RHO passes.

What should you bid now to describe your hand further?

a)	b)	c)	d)
♠ KQJ75	♠ AQJ864	♠ AQ985	♠ KQJ74
♥ 64	♥ QJ2	♥ AJ94	♥ 1053
♦ J53	♦ 76	♦ 53	♦ KQJ
♣ J72	♣ 95	♣ 86	♣ J9

a) 2S. Minimum.

b) 3S. Non-minimum, with a 6-card suit

c) 2H. This shows 5–4 distribution in your two suits.

d) 2NT. At least 11pts, with one and a half or two stoppers opponent's suit.

Once you have shown your hand, if partner returns to your original suit at the lowest available level, that ends the auction.

Jump overcalls

Many aggressive players these days, especially at duplicate bridge, play that to jump when overcalling your suit, shows a weak hand (5–9pts) and a 6-card suit.

However, it more common when playing social bridge or Teams, to play Intermediate strength jump overcalls.

These bids always promise a 6-card suit of good quality, with approximately 10–14pts. In response, partner can use an UCB with 10pts or more, and 2-card support or better but, usually, partner will passe or raise your suit.

An overcall where you jump two levels is a **Pre-Emptive Overcall**. This shows a 7-card suit of good quality, but only 5–9pts. It should be used mainly when your side is not vulnerable.

Opponents vulnerable, your side not. Your RHO opens 1D. What should you bid here?

a)	b)	c)	d)
♠ 75	♠ KQJ10763	♠ 98	♠ Q1087
♥ AKJ1096	♥ 932	♥ AQJ96	♥ A94
♦ 942	♦ 932	♦ 76	♦ 2
♣ A8	♣ J104	♣ AKJ5	♣ AKQ93

a) 2H. A perfect Jump Overcall. Notice the high quality of the suit.

b) 3S. A perfect Pre-emptive overcall. Quality of suit is paramount.

c) 1H. Not suitable for a double as you hold no spade support.

d) Double. You have support for all the other suits, and your singleton will be more useful if partner plays in hearts or spades, as she will be ruffing with the shorter holding in trumps.

Remember that the main purpose of overcalling is to hope that partner can support you and form a barrage to push your opponents too high or, possibly, steal the contract and go one or two down to stop them from making their contract. When your side hold the minority of points, that is the best you can do.

When it turns out that your partner holds a good hand (and he uses an UCB) and your side may have the majority of points, you then want to bid accurately, to try to reach the best contract for your side.

All competitive bidding is judged best by assessing how many cards you and your partner hold between you (TTP) and bidding the same number or tricks quickly to cut out opposition bidding. When non-vulnerable, you can choose to bid one trick more than the number of cards you have between you.

1NT overcall

Some people play this shows 16–18pts, some 15–17pts. I prefer the former.

It shows a balanced-ish hand, with at least one, usually two, stoppers in the opponent's suit.

If the next opponent passes, Stayman and Transfers are available in response.

RHO opens 1D. What do you bid?

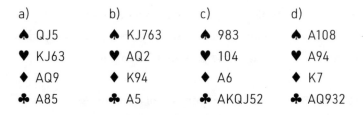

a)	b)	c)	d)
♠ QJ5	♠ KJ763	♠ 983	♠ A108
♥ KJ63	♥ AQ2	♥ 104	♥ A94
♦ AQ9	♦ K94	♦ A6	♦ K7
♣ A85	♣ A5	♣ AKQJ52	♣ AQ932

a) 1NT. A textbook example.

b) 1S. You only have one stopper in diamonds and you hold a 5-card major suit.

c) 1NT. Most would overcall 2C but, on the likely diamond lead, you have 7 tricks. If partner is weak, this might put your opponents off from bidding; if partner is slightly stronger, her points will lie in the major suits and 3NT could easily be made.

d) Double. A close decision, but with almost all the points in aces and kings, it looks better to aim for a suit contract that for no-trumps.

Partner responds as to an opening bid of 1NT but being aware that your range is not 12–14pts, but 16–18pts, so every bid requires 4pts fewer.

I have one last tip to impart here, and it is particularly important given the aggression shown by players these days:

Bidding after opponent overcalls 1NT

Your partner opens the bidding with 1H. LHO overcalls 1NT. What, if anything, should you bid on each of these hands?

a)	b)	c)	d)
♠ 75	♠ Q1076	♠ K95	♠ Q1087
♥ J1096	♥ 53	♥ 6	♥ J103
♦ 94	♦ K932	♦ J764	♦ AQ2
♣ AJ852	♣ J104	♣ KQJ108	♣ Q95

a) 2H. You have at least eight hearts between you and two doubletons. Support your partner and make your opponents bid at the 2 or 3-level.

b) Pass. The points are probably 20–20 between the two partnerships.

c) Double. Your side holds the majority of points and you know what you're going to lead against 1NT – K♣. This will almost inevitably lead to defeat for your opponent and a nice penalty for you.

d) Double. Your side holds the clear majority of points, so defeat them and collect your penalty.

Generally, do not change suit. Never support partner without 4-card support and shape.
With 10pts or more, always double for penalties.

Doubles and responses

Ninety-nine percent of the time, when you double (with your partner not having made a positive bid) you are short in your opponent's suit, with 3 or 4-card support for all the other suits.

We will look at the rare exceptions at the end.

RHO opens 1C. What should you bid here?

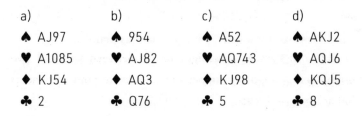

a)	b)	c)	d)
♠ AJ97	♠ 954	♠ A52	♠ AKJ2
♥ A1085	♥ AJ82	♥ AQ743	♥ AQJ6
♦ KJ54	♦ AQ3	♦ KJ98	♦ KQJ5
♣ 2	♣ Q76	♣ 5	♣ 8

a) Double. Opening hand, support for all the other suits, shortage in opponent's suit.

b) Pass. You are not short in your opponent's suit. Only compete on distributional hands.

c) 1H. With a 5-card major suit, you will do better to overcall the suit initially and, if your opponents' support clubs, you can always double on the next round. That would then be a take-out double, showing 3 or 4-card support for the unbid suits as well as five hearts.

d) Double. There is no upper limit to your strength.

When your opponents have bid two different suits, only double if you are at least 5–4 in the other two suits. If your opponents have changed suit at the 2-level, only double with 5–5 distribution or, if only 5–4, 16pts plus. Be aware that, as always, if you can at the 1 or 2-level, bid a 5-card major suit opposed to doubling.

Responding to a take-out double

I am always amazed how bad people are at doing this. Please be certain that you study this section as, if you aren't fluent, it will really adversely affect your competitive bidding abilities.

This is how to think when your partner has doubled:

Assume that your partner holds a 4–4–4–1 hand – with the singleton in opponent's suit.

Assume that partner holds 12/13pts.

Partner may not be this exact shape, and maybe stronger than minimum, but these assumptions will really help you to judge at what level you should bid.

When partner doubles, she is asking you not only to tell her your longest suit, but at what level you would like to play. This means that:

In response to a take-out double you must bid as many of your best suit as you think you can make.

LHO opens 1C; your partner doubles; RHO passes. With what should you respond here?

a)	b)	c)	d)
♠ 972	♠ KJ95	♠ A52	♠ 108632
♥ 85	♥ Q32	♥ AQ764	♥ AQJ
♦ 754	♦ Q86	♦ 98	♦ AJ10
♣ 97632	♣ 1074	♣ 653	♣ 87

a) Aaaaahhhh! You have to bid something: 1D or 1S will do. Both responses show 0–5/6pts.

b) 2S. You must distinguish between having nothing, and having, roughly, 7–9pts.

c) 3H. You have a 5-card suit and 10pts – almost an opening hand, so almost bid game.

d) 4S. Opening hand opposite opening hand equals game. Bid it. It doesn't matter about your poor suit quality: partner will probably hold high-quality spades.

Some more problems. Again, LHO opens 1C; your partner doubles; RHO passes. With what should you respond here?

e)	f)	g)	h)
♠ J972	♠ 107	♠ AK52	♠ Q108632
♥ K5	♥ 92	♥ AQ87	♥ AQJ
♦ AQJ4	♦ AQ8653	♦ 98	♦ 3
♣ 972	♣ AJ10	♣ 653	♣ 876

e) 3S. Always pick the major ahead of the minor.

With very weak hands, if you have five of a minor, and four of a major, bid the longer suit. With strong hands, say 10pts or more, bid a 4-card major ahead of a 5-card minor suit.

f) 3NT. Not the response your partner wants to hear because she hoped you'd have an 8-card major-suit fit but, as you have a fit in a minor suit and two stoppers in the opener's suit, it's the right contract. Do not worry about the major suits: your partner has strongly suggested four cards in each and will have values there.

g) 2C. An Unassuming Cue-bid. See below for full explanation – but you already know it asks partner to describe his hand further.

h) 4S. Bid up opposite take-out doubles. Your shape more than makes up for your slight lack of points: always bear this in mind.

Unassuming cue-bid in response to a take-out double

Look back at example g) above.

You have both major suits and an opening hand, so you have to bid a game contract. It would be very sad if you punted 4H and partner only held 3-card support, but 4-card spade support – and vice versa.

That is why, when you have sufficient points to play at the level to which you are forcing your partner to bid (usually about 7/8pts or more), *with two suits of the same rank*, you use an UCB to check that you definitely find your 8-card fit.

Your two possible suits will be the same rank – the two majors, or two minors – as, if you held one major suit and one minor suit, you would always bid the major.

South opens 1D:

a)		b)	
West	**East**	**West**	**East**
♠ AK75	♠ K1096	♠ AQ5	♠ J1062
♥ K106	♥ A852	♥ AKJ8	♥ Q1075
♦ 93	♦ AJ	♦ 62	♦ AK4
♣ K984	♣ J74	♣ Q1097	♣ 73
Dbl	2D	Dbl	2C
2S	**4S**	3H	**4H**

a) East doesn't know which major suit to bid, so he uses an UCB. Partner knows he needs to choose between the major suits, so he bids his 4-card major. East, with an opening hand, raises to game.

b) East neither knows which major suit to bid, nor how high his side can bid. He uses an UCB and West jumps to 3H, showing a better than minimum hand, say 15pts or more, and East can now bid game.

If, following an UCB, the doubler holds four cards in both the possible suits, he just bids his stronger 4-card suit.

Doubler's rebid following partner's response

When you have made a take-out double, if partner uses an UCB to force you to describe your hand further, you must do so.

Otherwise, unless you are stronger than you promised, say with 15pts or more, you will pass whatever your partner responds.

LHO opens 1S, you double. RHO passes; partner responds 3C. LHO passes. What do you say now?

a)	b)	c)	d)
♠ 75	♠ 86	♠ 2	♠ 5
♥ K1096	♥ AJ95	♥ AQJ6	♥ AKQ9
♦ K42	♦ AQ32	♦ AJ74	♦ A852
♣ AQJ8	♣ K74	♣ K953	♣ A763

a) Pass. You have lovely clubs, but a minimum point count, and poor shape.

b) Pass. You are not minimum, but you only have 3-card club support.

c) 4C. You are stronger than you promised with 4-card support. Invite partner to bid 5C.

d) 5C. Great fit, lots of aces and kings, lovely shape; must be worth a bash.

> *It is partner's responsibility to bid up in*
> *response to your take-out double.*
> *Unless partner uses an UCB, you will pass whatever she*
> *bids, unless you are markedly stronger than the hand*
> *your partner is assuming you hold: 4–4–4–1, 12/13pts.*

Rare use of double to show very strong hands

These examples occur very rarely but, because they show very strong hands, you need to know when to use them, and to recognise them when your partner bids this way.

Please read again the last italicised paragraph above.

When you respond to a take-out double, you partner will usually pass, occasionally raise your suit. She will never bid her own suit, or bid no-trumps – unless she is very strong.

The two occasions when you use double to show a very strong hand are when you hold a balanced hand with 19–22pts: with this, you double initially and, over the inevitable minimum response from partner, you bid NTs at the lowest available level; when you hold a hand with a 6-card suit (very rarely, a solid 5-card suit) with 16/17pts or more.

When you are too strong to overcall, you double initially and, over the inevitable minimum response from partner, bid your own suit at the lowest available level (or if you think you have nine tricks in your own hand, at the 3-level).

Why do I say over the "inevitable minimum response from partner"?

An opponent has opened the bidding, you have 16/17pts or more – it is very likely that your partner's hand falls into the 0–5/6pts minimum response. Remain aware that your partner could hold a Yarborough (zero points).

Your RHO opens 1C; you double; LHO passes; partner responds 1S; RHO passes.

What can you bid now?

a)	b)	c)
♠ KJ75	♠ AQ5	♠ A2
♥ K1096	♥ AJ106	♥ AQJ986
♦ AK42	♦ QJ2	♦ AQ
♣ 8	♣ AQ6	♣ 953

a) 2S. You have a slightly better than minimum take-out double, so raise to 2S (remember that partner is showing 0–5/6pts with her 1S response – don't get over-excited).

b) 1NT. You were too strong to overcall 1NT (and a 2NT overcall would have been an Unusual NT Overcall), so you double first and then rebid no-trumps. This shows 19–22pts, with at least one stopper in the opponent's suit.

c) 2H. You were too strong to overcall 2H or 3H, so you doubled first, and then rebid your suit. This shows usually a 6-card suit, similar to a Strong 2 Opening, with about 16pts plus.

Double of 1NT

If you double an opponent's opening bid of 1NT, this is for penalties and I advise that your partner always passes (unless the opponents escape 1NT into a long suit, when your partner might double for penalties, or bid suits of her own).

The types of hand on which you might double a 1NT opening would be:

A balanced hand with a good 16pts or more;

A distributional hand where, being on lead, you expect to make at least seven tricks in defence.

RHO opens 1NT. You hold:

a)	b)	c)	d)
♠ A75	♠ A6	♠ AKQJ87	♠ Q82
♥ AJ10	♥ 1084	♥ J5	♥ A54
♦ KQJ9	♦ 32	♦ K63	♦ KJ7
♣ Q86	♣ AKQJ53	♣ A4	♣ AJ63

a) Double. You know what to lead – K♦ – and, on average, your side will hold the majority of points.

b) Double. You are on lead, and can take seven tricks. You hold 14pts and two more for the fifth and sixth clubs, and half a point for 10♥. If opponents escape into hearts, you can later bid 3C.

c) Double. Much better then overcalling 2S or 3S, go for the penalty. If the opponents escape into another suit, you will bid spades subsequently.

d) Pass. You haven't sufficient points and you have no idea what you might lead.

Once a member of your side makes a penalty double, all subsequent doubles by your side are also for penalties. If you hold a balanced double and partner doubles something bid by the opposition, just pass. If your double was based on a 6-card suit or longer, then your hand is far less defensive than partner might have assumed, so bid your suit.

I am often asked what the right action might be once opponents have opened a weak 1NT. It is a notoriously difficult judgement to make, especially at duplicate pairs. That's just one more reason to love playing Weak NT.

♠ ♥
♦ ♣

Trying to be amenable to your partner is a vital technique at cut-in bridge. These days most people play social bridge with their friends, or duplicate with their chosen partner but, in the old days, club bridge partnerships would be decided by cutting for partners. You just had to make the best of whomever chance joined you to.

A middle-aged, upright, French lady cut me when I was still a teenager. She couldn't hide her disgust.

"What," she demanded in an imperious, thick accent, "do you want to play?"

"Whatever you like," I said eagerly.

"You choose," she told me. "Strong or Weak NT?"

"I prefer weak."

"Non,' she declared. "Strong is better."

I agreed and then we discussed Stayman.

"I'm happy to play it, but it's up to you," I said.

"It's up to you," she told me, jangling her charm bracelets.

"Let's play Stayman."

"Non! It's not so good."

"Okay…"

"Now, do you want transfers?" she enquired.

"I'm happy with whatever you'd like."

"You tell me," she insisted.

"I like red-suit transfers,' I say.

"Non. No transfers."

I took a deep breath.

"What else would you like?" she persisted.

"Really," I told her, "I'm happy to play whatever you want. Why don't you just tell me what you'd like us to play?"

She laughed scornfully, threw back her head, and said:

"Non, non… I always let the *weaker* player choose!"

The partnership did not fare well, not least because of a truly gobsmacking play my partner made later on.

In 3NT, she needed just three diamond tricks for the vulnerable game contract.

She carefully led 2♦ from hand and, when West played low, expertly finessed with 10♦!

♦ AQ10

♦ 954   ♦ J873

♦ K62

This is what expert players cannot understand and what teachers have to appreciate: massively underestimating a bridge player's ability (including one's own) never leads to disappointment.

Bidding gadgets and conventions

These are primarily for more experienced players, regular partnerships, and duplicate bridge players, and information can be found in many of my other books, perhaps most fully in "Control The Bidding."

If I were to recommend certain conventions you might like to adopt, they would be as follows, roughly in order of preference:

Negative Doubles
Michaels Cue-bids
Weak 2 Openers in the major suits
Transfers
Asptro: a conventional defence to 1NT.

And other advanced understandings:

Protective Bidding and Balancing
High-level competitive bidding
The Law of Total Tricks.

In addition to those already described in this section, such as Roman Key-Card Blackwood, three bidding conventions that I think you should play – and which I would expect anyone who claims to be "pretty good" at bridge to understand – would be:

Stayman
Fourth Suit Forcing
Unusual NT Overcall.

Let's take a quick look at each of these to introduce you to them or, more likely, just to double-check that you have the salient points at the forefront of your mind.

Stayman

Opposite an opening bid of 1NT, you use this gadget to check for a 4–4 major suit fit.

To use Stayman in this position (and the others described) your hand must contain one 4-card major suit, or both.

> *To use Stayman, your hand must contain at least one exactly 4-card major suit.*

To use Stayman, you must be able to cope with any response the opener may give you.

In response to an opening bid of 1NT, a bid of 2C asks whether partner's hand contains a 4-card major suit.

If partner holds four spades, she bids 2S;
With four hearts, she bids 2H.
Hold both majors containing four cards, she first responds 2H;
With no 4-card major suit, she responds 2D.

Let's look at some examples. Partner opens 1NT (12–14), the next opponent passes.

a)	b)	c)	d)
♠ 75	♠ AJ84	♠ AQ74	♠ KJ5
♥ K653	♥ AJ95	♥ J862	♥ AQ973
♦ K1097	♦ 32	♦ J74	♦ 52
♣ AQJ	♣ J104	♣ 53	♣ A86

a) Respond 2C. If partner bids 2H, raise to 4H. If partner bids 2D or 2S, bid what you would have bid had you not used Stayman in the first place: 3NT.

b) Respond 2C. If partner bids 2H or 2S, raise to 3H or 3S to show 11/12pts; if partner bids 2D, bid what you would have bid had you not used Stayman in the first place: 2NT.

c) Pass. If partner bids 2D, you do not have a bid, since 2NT promises 11/12pts.

d) 3H (or, if playing Transfers, 2D). Your hand does not contain a 4-card major suit, so to use Stayman would be incorrect.

> *Opposite a 12–14pt 1NT opener you normally*
> *require 11pts or more to use Stayman.*

This allows you to return to 2NT (or more) if your partner does not have a 4–4 match with you.

But, there are some exceptions:

e) 2C. You can use Stayman with 0pts+ when you hold 5/4 in the major suits. If partner bids 2H or 2S, you pass; if she bids 2D, you return to your 5-card major suit at the 2-level, where it is still a weak take-out.

f) 2C. Here, you can pass any response from partner: 2S, 2H and 2D. She will be pretty shocked when you pass 2D but, once she sees your hand, she will realise that you have made the perfect bid.

> *When you are 5–4 in the major suits, either way around, or you are 4–4 in the majors and also a 5-card diamond suit, you may use Stayman with no points at all since, whatever response partner gives, you can still sign off at the 2-level. This is still a weak take-out.*

Not everyone who claims to play Stayman knows this, so it may surprise some less experienced players.

g) 2C. To everyone at the table, this sounds like you are using Stayman but, whatever response you receive from your partner, you will then rebid 3C (now explaining that you were not using Stayman), but making a weak take-out into clubs.

You will almost always have a 6-card club suit and a hand of 9pts or fewer (with more points, no-trumps may still be the right denomination). Partner will pass.

When you play Stayman, you must also remain alert should you open 1NT with both majors and partner employs Stayman:

h) | **West** | **East** |
|---|---|
| ♠ KQ75 | ♠ AJ84 |
| ♥ AK83 | ♥ 62 |
| ♦ J94 | ♦ KQ73 |
| ♣ 52 | ♣ QJ4 |
| 1NT | 2C |
| 2H | 3NT |
| **4S** | |

East uses Stayman, West correctly responds 2H. When East correctly rebids 3NT, showing 13pts+, West should realise that to use Stayman East promised a 4-card major and, as it isn't hearts, it must be spades. So, she converts to the 4–4 spade fit.

Some people might ask why East didn't bid spades? The answer is simple: to bid a suit opposite 1NT promises five cards and, anyway, it so simple and logical this way: East has promised a 4-card major when he used Stayman. If it isn't hearts, it must be spades!

Check with a new partner, but most people also play Stayman in these situations too:

In response to 2NT opening bid (requires 4/5pts or more)

In response to the sequence 2C, followed by a 2NT re-bid (requiring 1/2pts upwards)

In response to Protective bids of 1NT and 2NT (requires sufficient points to be cope with any

response partner might give you).

Fourth suit forcing

I consider this gadget as just part of bridge, since it is absolutely vital if you want to bid accurately.

Here, I present only an abbreviated version, to ensure that you understand the basic principle. This wonderful bidding understanding can be further studied in my other books.

Your partner opens 1H, you respond 1S. Partner rebids 2C. What should you bid now?

a)	b)	c)	d)
♠ KQ752	♠ KQ752	♠ AK864	♠ AJ973
♥ 83	♥ J6	♥ KJ8	♥ 6
♦ AQ9	♦ Q84	♦ A75	♦ KQJ108
♣ Q64	♣ AJ3	♣ 92	♣ K5

a) 3NT. Three suits have been bid. You hold two stoppers in the unbid suit, so playing in no trumps seems correct. You hold an opening hand opposite and opening hand, so bid game.

b) 2D. You have an opening hand, but you do not hold two stoppers in the unbid suit, so to bid no-trumps now would be risky (and wrong). Instead, bid the fourth suit, which is

Fourth Suit Forcing, asking your partner to describe her hand further.

c) 2D. Fourth Suit Forcing. This time, you know that you hold an 8-card fit in hearts but, since partner could still hold up to about 18pts, you do not know whether to play in game or look for a slam. Use 4SF to ask partner to describe her hand further and then support hearts subsequently – this shows around 14pts or more with 3-card heart support.

d) 3NT. Do not ever bid the fourth suit as a suggestion for trumps – just give up on that idea. It will probably never, ever occur in your lifetime that you want to play with the fourth suit mentioned as trumps. The hand is a misfit, you have the combined points for game – just bid it.

To use Fourth Suit Forcing you need to know that Game is on. Therefore, unless your partner has made a reverse, you require an opening hand to make this bid.

Having used 4SF, the auction becomes forcing to game – neither player may pass before a game contract has been bid.

The 4SF bid suggest that partner has something in the fourth suit, but not sufficiently good cards to bid NTs herself.

What you bid after partner has used 4SF

Partner has asked you to describe your hand further, and that is what you must do.

You have, so far, shown five cards in your first suit and four in your second suit.

If you hold a stopper (Jxxx, Qxx, Kx, Ax) in the fourth suit, rebid no-trumps. Between you and your partner, you should now hold sufficient protection to survive an attack on that suit from your opponents.

If you hold 5–5 in your two suits, bid the second suit again.

If you hold 6–5 in your two suits, jump rebid your second suit.

If you hold 6–4 in your two suits, jump rebid your first suit.

If you hold 3-card support for partner's first bid suit, bid that suit at the 3-level.

If you hold no extra shape and no values in the fourth suit, just rebid your first suit at the lowest available level and leave partner to make the further decisions.

There are other, even more accurate bids, that can be made, but those above are the most common and the most useful.

Let's see 4SF in action in a couple of examples:

a)		b)	
West	**East**	**West**	**East**
♠ K75	♠ AQJ62	♠ Q	♠ AJ862
♥ KQJ106	♥ A2	♥ AQ853	♥ 76
♦ 4	♦ Q53	♦ 74	♦ K83
♣ A932	♣ K74	♣ KQ874	♣ AJ5
1H	1S	1H	1S
2C	2D*	2C	2D*
3S	4NT	3C	4C
5H	**6S**	**5C**	

a) Following East's 2D 4SF bid, West bids partner's suit at the 3-level, showing 3-card support. East now knows that West is 5–4–3–1, with a singleton diamond. This encourages her to use RKCB and, on discovering that West holds two key cards, she bids the excellent slam.

b) Following East's 2D 4SF bid, West rebids her second suit, denying any honours in diamonds and showing 5–5 distribution. East now supports clubs. West, being minimum, simply bids game.

Fourth Suit Forcing shouldn't really need to be discussed: all decent players would assume that to bid the fourth suit would mean what I have described above. However, if you are playing with a new partner, or a new group of friends, it is worthwhile to discuss it.

Unusual NT

Standard overcalls of no-trumps usually show a strong hand, with two stoppers in the opponent's suit and a moderately balanced distribution (that might contain a long minor suit).

However, any strange, peculiar overcall of no-trumps is generally understood to be the Unusual NT Overcall (UNT).

The Unusual No-trump is a competitive device, ideally suited to finding a good sacrifice in 5C or 5D, to your opponents' major-suit game contract. It is therefore best employed when your side is not vulnerable.

This bid shows 5–5 or longer in the two lowest-ranking unbid suits. People play the strength requirements differently, but I would recommend around 10pts upwards, with as many as possible concentrated in the two long suits.

The success of a two-suited overcall will rest on the quality and texture of the two suits which, in both cases, must be high.

If your opponent(s) bid a major suit, the UNT Overcall shows both minors;

if your opponent(s) bid a minor suit, the UNT Overcall shows hearts and the other minor;

if your opponents bid two suits, the UNT Overcall shows the remaining two suits.

Your RHO opens 1H. What would you bid on each of these hands?

a)	b)	c)	d)
♠ 52	♠ J	♠ AK864	♠ 5
♥ 3	♥ Q7	♥ J8	♥ 7
♦ KQ1098	♦ K8753	♦ 5	♦ KQ1094
♣ AJ1098	♣ A6432	♣ QJ1092	♣ QJ10863

a) 2NT. A 1NT overcall would be natural, showing 16–18pts and a balanced, so you have to jump to make an Unusual NT Overcall. Note all values in your two suits, great texture to the suits.

b) Pass. Right shape, poor quality suits. A bad idea to use an UNT Overcall here.

c) 1S. You are 5–5, but the UNT Overcall shows the two lowest ranking unbid suits – and you don't have them. Start with 1S and see how the auction develops.

d) 2NT. Weak on points, but with 6–5 shape and great quality suits. Absolutely fine.

Imagine that your opponents bid 1S - 3S, and your partner bids 3NT. That is a pretty odd overcall of no-trumps, and it would indeed be an UNT Overcall, probably showing 6–5 in the two minor suits.

What about 1H-4H from your opponents, and partner bids 4NT. That is not RKCB, as neither of you have mentioned a suit, let alone agreed one. So, again, that is an UNT Overcall, definitely 6–5 this time, as partner is asking you to choose a minor suit at the 5-level.

Responding to an unusual NT overcall

If partner uses an UNT Overcall, and the next opponent passes, you have to bid.

There might be a time where it is right to pass, leaving your partner to play, but I have never seen an example, so better to remember that you are forced to bid.

If the next opponent bids, you do not have to make a bid.

As you do when responding to a take-out double, you must bid not only your preferred suit, but also bid at the maximum level you believe that your side can make since, unless she is much stronger than the 10pts and 5–5 distribution promised, partner will pass any response you make. LHO opens 1H; partner overcalls 2NT; RHO passes. With what do you respond?

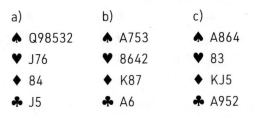

a)	b)	c)
♠ Q98532	♠ A753	♠ A864
♥ J76	♥ 8642	♥ 83
♦ 84	♦ K87	♦ KJ5
♣ J5	♣ A6	♣ A952

a) 3C. You have to choose between the minors and your clubs are better. Horrible, but it must be done.

b) 4D. Aces and kings, good cards in the minors and, if partner is 6–5, or stronger than she might be, game could still be on for your side. Ten tricks should be achievable, even if partner is minimum.

c) 5C. A double fit in clubs and diamonds, aces and a king; you will surely make ten tricks in the minor suits, and A♠.

Rebids having used an UNT overcall

You will usually pass whatever partner says and, even if the opponents bid on, you must not bid again unless you are much stronger, or more distributional, that you promised.

RHO opens 1S, you overcall 2NT; LHO passes. Partner responds 3D; RHO opponent bids 3H.

What, if anything, should you bid now?

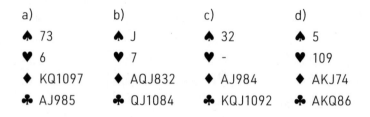

a)	b)	c)	d)
♠ 73	♠ J	♠ 32	♠ 5
♥ 6	♥ 7	♥ -	♥ 109
♦ KQ1097	♦ AQJ832	♦ AJ984	♦ AKJ74
♣ AJ985	♣ QJ1084	♣ KQJ1092	♣ AKQ86

a) Pass. You have shown your hand the first time. Partner has bid the minimum, and may only hold two diamonds. To bid again would be very bad.

b) 4D. You have six diamonds opposed to the five you promised; it is worth the risk to bid on.

c) 4C. Yes, partner chose diamonds, but you are showing your extra card in clubs. If partner held 2 diamonds and two clubs, you'd want to play in clubs.

d) Double. This shows about 15/16pts upwards, with defensive values and only 5–5 distribution. If partner has 3/4-card support, he can bid on to 4D or 5D but, holding only a doubleton in both suits, he now has the option to pass and penalise the opponents in their contract.

Following a bridge event, four of us went to supper at a smart restaurant in London. For some reason, that night, the service was appallingly slow, and it was well past 11pm before we reached pudding.

The obsequious waiter informed us that they had few of the menu options remaining, and this annoyed one of the ladies with us no end. She was of the view that she had been most unlucky at the bridge tournament, and that her bad day was continuing into the night.

She managed to keep her wits about her when the waiter said:

"What about coffee? We have expresso, cappuccino, latte, americano, cortado, filter or decaffeinated. Which," he said to our friend, "do you want?"

She didn't miss a beat.

"Instant."

Epilogue

At the bridge table, it is easy to think that you have done everything you could as declarer, or in defence but, often, there is something that you didn't spot, maybe didn't even know about. That's why bridge is such a fascinating game. To enjoy it to the full, I recommend keeping a constantly open mind and, if possible, review hands that you have played, so that you can check your thinking.

Anyone who is certain about anything at the green baize is probably deluded.

And that last sentence reminds me of my favourite aphorism, and one which I hope works both ways (although I suspect it doesn't). The philosopher, Bertrand Russell, claims that:

"The fundamental cause of the trouble is that in the modern world the stupid are *cocksure,* while the intelligent are *full of doubt.*"

Remain questioning, doubtful, logical, and modest and you will enjoy your bridge and so will the people with whom you play. Become hubristic and cocksure, and your game will suffer and no one will want to play with you.

I hope that, if you are a more experienced player, you still found points of interest in this tome. Remember that, at the bridge table, once you understand something, it is hard to imagine ever not comprehending it. I always try to remember how difficult this game is. Please try to do the same.

Good luck, and I hope you pick up some excellent cards.

Paul Mendelson

www.aceoftrumps.com

Acknowledgements

I would like to thank my editor and publisher, Duncan Proudfoot, for continuing to champion my writing, Rita Gallinari for wading through my original text and, amidst a sea of missing cards and unclear explanations, finding clarity and accuracy and you, my cherished students, for laughing anew each time you hear my old stories.